**Stuart Hillard** is the best-selling author of six stunning sewing books and one of the most recognisable figures in the industry. With a career spanning over twenty-five years, Stuart has designed hundreds of sewing projects, sharing his knowledge with thousands of students. His versatile designs reflect Stuart's interest in a variety of bag-making methods, combining traditional piecing with innovative techniques from across the world.

Stuart is part of the presenter team on Sewing Street TV and a well-loved and sought-after teacher and speaker. As Patron of the Quilters' Guild of the British Isles, he cherishes the opportunity to support and encourage quilt making whilst helping to preserve the UK's quilting heritage. Stuart designs fabric ranges for Lewis & Irene and yarn collections for Stylecraft Yarns. He is the author of *Bags for Life; Sew Fabulous; Use Scraps, Sew Blocks, Make 100 Quilts; Simple Shapes, Stunning Quilts; Quilts from the Country;* and *Make 100 Bags.*

When not immersed in the sewing world, Stuart enjoys cooking, spending time with friends, and helping to run the family farm in North Yorkshire with his husband, Charlie.

# MAKE 100 BAGS

Use Scraps, Sew Fabric

# MAKE 100 BAGS

STUART HILLARD

PAVILION

This book is dedicated to the memory of my beloved parents, Rex and Rosemary Hillard.

Pavilion
An imprint of HarperCollins*Publishers* Ltd
1 London Bridge Street
London SE1 9GF

www.harpercollins.co.uk

HarperCollins*Publishers*
Macken House
39/40 Mayor Street Upper,
Dublin 1
D01 C9W8
Ireland

10 9 8 7 6 5 4 3 2 1

First published in Great Britain by Pavilion
An imprint of HarperCollins*Publishers* 2025



Stuart Hillard asserts the moral right to be identified as the author of this work. A catalogue record of this book is available from the British Library.

ISBN 9780008584931

This book contains FSC™ certified paper and other controlled sources to ensure responsible forest management.

For more information visit: www.harpercollins.co.uk/green

Publishing Director: Laura Russell
Editor: Shamar Gunning
Copyeditor: Corinne Colvin
Editorial Assistant: Daisy Gudmunsen
Design Manager: Alice Kennedy-Owen
Junior Designer: Lily Wilson
Layout Designer: James Boast
Production Controller: Grace O'Byrne
Photographer: Rachel Whiting
Illustrators: Kang Chen, Virginia Romo
Prop Stylist: Amy Neason
Proofreader: Sarah Epton

Printed in China by RR Donnelley

# CONTENTS

# HOW TO USE THIS BOOK... AND HOW TO MAKE 100 BAGS!

I've been sewing and making things for as long as I can remember. One of my earliest childhood memories is of making a small felt bag from a rectangle of folded fabric. I took my tiny bag on holiday, and everywhere I went the bag went. That little bag was one of my first proper makes and it was both practical and beautiful – the perfect combination of use and ornament.

Bags are one of the most fun things to sew; they are quick projects (most take less than a day to complete) and there are lots of short processes so, if you're someone like me who gets bored easily, you will stay on your toes throughout! Bags are also incredibly satisfying to make because as fun as they are to create, the real joy comes in the wearing and the using. I design bag patterns to be practical, but I also heartily approve of a bit of mix-and-match, so once you get the hang of things don't be afraid to change up the straps, the pockets or the closure to make the bag patterns in this book work for you.

When I started planning this book I wanted to create a collection of beautiful, useful, easy-to-make and fabulous-to-own bags that would have you running to your sewing machine. I aimed to create bag patterns that were simple to cut out and easy to sew, with a minimum of fuss and maximum bang for your buck. I really love designing projects that look impressive but are deceptively easy to construct. I challenged myself to design twenty all-new bag patterns that everyone would love. I also made sure to include tutorials on every skill you'll need to complete every single bag – perfect for complete beginners, as well as seasoned bag-makers.

But I still wanted to take those bag patterns further!

I set out to explore the possibilities of combining patchwork and quilting traditions with my new bag patterns; a mix-and-match approach that would see the number of design possibilities skyrocket.

Each pattern in this book is made and photographed in the 'simply fabric' method, no patchwork as such, maybe with a little contrast on the base or flap – the perfect way to make the bag if you have half a metre of suitable fabric or enjoy showing off the beauty of a carefully chosen print.

But what if you're a scrap quilter/hoarder like me? What if your cupboards, wardrobes and under-bed storage are full of the remnants of dressmaking, quilting and crafts? That's where the patchwork methods come in!

You get to choose from four patchwork traditions to switch up every pattern: explore hand-sewn English paper piecing to create mosaic patchwork from a variety of sizes of hexagons – a perfect way to use up beautiful scraps! Give string piecing a go: it's a traditional patchwork technique that uses long, thin strips of fabrics and more latterly the fancy selvedges from quilting cottons to create new 'fabric' – you can literally turn rags into riches! Or why not explore one of the most iconic methods of patchwork from Japan. 'Boro' is a simple technique of patching fabric with roughly cut, or even torn, pieces of fabric, held down with beautiful running stitches in simple or intricate designs. Finally, ditch the rules and liberate your piecing with a spot of 'improv' or crazy quilting. Rooted in tradition but surprisingly modern and fresh, this is a fun technique that could literally use up every scrap you own!

Each bag is photographed made in simple fabric and a patchwork method, with the remaining three methods illustrated to give you some ideas. I want you to use the patterns and the methods as a glorious springboard to your own creativity. Make every bag your way, as unique as you are!

In *Make 100 Bags* you have: five methods (simply fabric, English paper piecing, string piecing, boro and improv) x twenty patterns = 100 bags!

brother

# MATERIALS

For almost every bag featured in this book you'll need the same basic components: fabric for the outer bag and handles, fabric for the lining and inner pockets, some kind of stiffening or padding agent that sits inside the bag, and some kind of fastening. You'll also need some thread to hold the whole thing together. That's it ... at its simplest. The way you use that fabric, the patterns you pick, the colours you choose and the way you put it all together are what really makes every bag unique. The rest is all bells and whistles: fancy metalware, locking mechanisms, strap sliders, feet and zips – there's a huge amount of choice out there, and although there are a few extra skills to learn in order to add these to your bags, the results are worth it! The right accessories on a bag can make all the difference and elevate your makes beyond your wildest dreams! This is the bit most of us get really excited about; it's the bit that shows most and the part that can show off your personal sense of style, match an outfit or show the world who you are. It's also the part of the bag that needs to stand up to the rigours of whatever you'll use it for, so it's worth keeping this in mind too when you're choosing your materials.

# FABRICS FOR THE OUTER BAG

## 1. COTTON FABRICS

I love using cotton fabrics, and in particular quilt-weight cottons for bag-making. The colours, patterns, scale and styles seem almost endless, and they are readily available and very easy to work with. If I'm making a bag that is 'whole-cloth', I'll generally use two or three different fabrics to keep the bag looking interesting, perhaps mixing a large-scale print with a stripe and a blender or small-scale print for added interest. Look out for more unusual cotton fabrics like African wax prints, shibori dyed cottons and waxed cottons. All are easy to sew, wear and wash well, and are a great choice for beginners and experienced makers alike.

## 2. COTTON CANVAS

A heavier and slightly coarser weave than quilt-weight cottons, this tends to come in plain colours but is a brilliant fabric for bag-making. It's a little heavier and so will hold its shape rather well. Still use the recommended interfacing or foam and you will be rewarded with an easy-to-make bag, particularly encouraging if you are at the start of your bag-making odyssey.

But there are lots of other fabrics available for bag-making, too.

## 3. TAPESTRY FABRICS

I enjoy using upholstery-style tapestry fabrics, which are a bit thicker and heavier than quilting cottons. This robustness makes them great for heavier-duty bags like rucksacks and travel bags. You may even find that padding or interfacing is unnecessary as the fabric is strong and firm enough on its own. The extra thickness does make these fabrics more suitable for larger, simpler bags. Tapestry fabrics are often reversible too, so if you're not planning on lining your bag they can be very useful.

## 4. FAUX LEATHER

Faux leather is a great choice for bag-making. It's soft, supple and very easy to sew – just use a walking foot or a non-stick foot when you are topstitching, as the fabric can stick to the underside of the machine presser foot and make sewing tricky. Faux leather can be used with or without interfacing/wadding, but it looks particularly smart when it is quilted, and lends bags a very tailored and professional look.

## 5. DENIM, CORDUROY AND VELVET

These are traditionally thought of as dressmaking fabrics. However, they can all be used to make fabulous bags. Just consider the weight of the fabric you're using and adjust your interfacings accordingly. Don't be afraid to mix your dressmaking staples with quilters cottons – just interface the lighter fabric to bring it to the same weight, then proceed as normal.

## 6. CLEAR VINYL

This can be very useful in bags when a 'window' is required. Plain, coloured or glittered versions are available, and it's very easy to sew with a non-stick foot on your machine. I find vinyl particularly useful for pockets where I need to see inside. The edges can't be hemmed in the traditional way, so are 'bound' like the edges of a quilt.

## 7. OIL CLOTH AND CORK FABRIC

Also look out for oil cloth/plastic-coated fabrics; these have a brilliantly useful wipeable surface. Or use cork fabric, which was an absolute revelation the first time I used it. It is surprisingly soft and flexible, and very easy to cut and sew. It is also naturally wipeable, so great for items that might get grubby easily.

11
9
12
Vlieseline H250
10
10
7
4
3

## 8. LINING FABRICS

The lining of your bags and the outer pockets deserve every bit as much consideration as the main attraction. You'll be seeing the lining every time you go into a pocket or the interior of your bag, so make sure it's a fabric you love and one that complements or enhances the bag – don't treat the lining as an afterthought! Quilt-weight cotton, cotton poplin, polycottons and lawn cloth fabrics all make great bag linings. I usually go for something fairly light in colour and not too patterned so that things are easy to find! If you need your lining to be waterproof or wipeable, use a ripstop, waxed or plastic-coated cotton, or recycle a shower curtain!

## 9. SHOULDER STRAPS AND HANDLES

If you're making your own, then you have a few choices. Use the same fabric as the main bag or use a coordinating stripe or pattern to enhance or contrast with the main bag. Look out for cotton webbing in a suitable weight, width and colour, and use nylon webbing for even more durability. It's generally available by the metre and I tend to buy 3 metres at a time, which will make short handles for several bags, or handles and a shoulder strap for one bag. Keep a look-out for really fancy brocade or patterned webbing; I'll sometimes design a bag colour scheme around a length of fancy webbing in my stash. You can also use faux leather, cork or oil cloth for your straps and handles, but these fabrics require slightly different handling. I also keep my eyes open for ready-made handles and straps, and have used them a number of times in this book. They add a very professional look and make the finished bag very stylish; they are also a rather lovely 'quick finish' for a bag.

## 10. THREAD

Always, always use quality thread; after all, it's the stuff that holds your project together, and really good-quality thread will also run through your sewing machine better. There are cotton, polyester and blends available in a plethora of colours, and all are perfectly serviceable for bag-making. I like to use linen thread for sewing on buttons and buckles, but also look out for extra-strong upholstery thread, which comes in a range of neutral shades and is really good for providing super-strong hand- or machine-sewn seams.

For some of the projects in this book you'll be doing some hand sewing. For English paper piecing I recommend a 50-weight, or better still an 80-weight hand-sewing thread, if you can get it – the finer the thread, the better the results! You might also need some sashiko thread for hand quilting or 'boro' stitching, or you can use several strands of embroidery floss.

## 11. CORD

Whether it's 3 or 4mm cotton piping cord to cover and enhance a seam or more decorative cords to use as a drawstring, cord deserves its place in your bag-maker's stash. I generally buy at least 5 metres of decorative cord, and piping cord tends to come in at least 10 metres at a time. I never want to run out and although you might be blessed with a local shop that has all kinds of everything, that won't help when you get the urge to make a bag at 10pm at night!

## 12. INTERFACINGS, WADDINGS AND FOAMS

If the main fabrics and linings are the body, then the interfacing, wadding or foam is the skeleton. There is a wide variety of interfacings, waddings and foams that live inside our bags, nestled between the outer and lining and often fused, stitched or quilted into place. These hidden layers are what give our bags structure and shape, and without them a lot of bags would be shapeless and floppy – imagine a body with no skeleton!

As a general rule, I will cut the interfacing, wadding or foam at least ¼" smaller on all sides than the fabric. I don't want multiple layers of extra bulk in the seam allowances where it does no good and just gets in the way of a great finish.

**13. IN-R-FORM/FUSIBLE FOAM** is my go-to when I need a very structured bag with a padded feel but one that is still very lightweight. Fusible foam comes in single- and double-sided fusible and non-fusible versions. Cut a single layer at a time.

**14. VOLUME FLEECE** like H640 and H630 from Vlieseline comes in a variety of weights and may be fusible or not. It's a little bit like interfacing with a thin layer of batting or wadding attached to it. It's great for adding padding and soft structure to a bag without adding weight.

**15. QUILT BATTING** can be used for giving a soft, padded feel to a bag, and you can choose between cotton, polyester or a mixture. It won't add much in the way of structure, but if you want to make something softly padded it's ideal.

**16. THERMOLAM/THERMAL INSULATING** is a great choice when you want heat retention or insulation, so it's ideal for lunch bags, picnic bags and water-bottle carriers. Any batting or wadding will insulate to a certain extent, but Thermolam and thermal insulating batting have a special construction and materials that make them extra-insulating.

**DECOVIL** is a type of interfacing that is very firm and stiff, and feels very much like leather. It is bonded to the wrong side of fabric and makes it rigid – perfect for very structured bags and boxes, especially when you want a strong but thin structure. It can also be used in conjunction with volume fleece or quilt batting to get a padded but very firm finish.

**DECOVIL LIGHT** has a very similar handle to Decovil but is lighter and not so rigid. It still produces very firm results but with more flexibility.

**FUSIBLE INTERFACING** is a great choice as it is widely available and comes in different weights: light, medium and heavy, depending on the level of structure required. Medium-weight fusible interfacing is a great standby and can be used for shoulder straps and handles. For the vast majority of bags, I use medium-weight fusible interfacing on the lining; this creates a lovely structure to the lining and stops it from sagging into the bag. It also adds extra support to the whole bag. I keep the interfacing out of the seam allowances as much as I can by cutting my interfacing ¼" or more smaller than the fabric.

**'WAIST-SHAPER'** is a great alternative to interfacing for bag handles and shoulder straps, and it's fusible too! Originally designed to stiffen waistbands in dressmaking, it's also perfect for bag-making. It comes in a standard 3" width that can be trimmed to narrower widths. This is my favourite product to make shoulder straps and handles from when I'm using fabrics like cork and faux leather. Both materials are hard to 'turn through' a sewn tube, so instead fuse a layer of Waist-Shaper to the flat-strap fabric and fold the edges in to make a neatened strap, then topstitch down both sides to create a perfect strap or handle.

# EQUIPMENT

## 1. SEWING MACHINE

A sturdy sewing machine is going to be the most essential piece of kit in your bag-making journey. It doesn't need to be a fancy one; you'll mostly use a straight stitch and, footwise, a basic zigzag foot, a zipper foot and a walking foot should cover most jobs. The most important thing about the machine is that it is sturdy and well maintained. Bag-making involves sewing through heavy and thick layers, so a good motor is essential.

## 2. TEFLON OR NON-STICK FOOT

If you are planning on making bags from oil cloth, faux leather or vinyl, I recommend investing in one of these as the surface will resist 'sticking' to the fabrics and cause tiny, unattractive stitches.

## 3. MACHINE NEEDLES

Use good-quality machine needles and keep a range of sizes handy – I like size 90 or 100 for bag-making – and make sure you use a new needle for every project, not just when you break one! If you're having issues sewing thick layers and your machine is skipping stitches, increase the size of your needle (the higher the number, the thicker the needle). I like to use Schmetz universal needles or a Microtex size 70 for precision patchwork and piecing.

## 4. SEAM RIPPER

The tool we all love to hate ... no one likes unpicking seams, but it is ten times harder without one of these handy little rippers!

## 5. HAND-SEWING NEEDLES AND NEEDLE THREADER

Useful for hand sewing the gap in a lining closed, sewing on a button or press stud, or for making English paper piecing. I like 'sharps' and really recommend John James hand-sewing needles. Also, get yourself some sturdier embroidery needles and quilting needles if you're having a go at boro or if you want to hand quilt your bags. A needle threader is essential too ... life's too short to waste 5 minutes trying to thread a needle!

## 6. SCISSORS

Ideally, you should have two pairs: a medium or large pair for general cutting out, and a small fine-tipped pair of embroidery scissors for detail cutting and snipping. Make sure you keep your scissors just for cutting fabric. It's also very useful to have pinking shears to trim seam allowances and notch fabric around curves.

## 7. THREAD SNIPS

These are ideal for cutting threads ... use these and not your scissors!

## 8. ROTARY CUTTER/RULER/MAT

A rotary cutter is a great way to cut strips, squares or rectangles. Multiple layers can be cut at once and the pieces are very accurate.

## 9. TRACING/TISSUE PAPER

Use dressmakers tissue paper to create paper patterns. It's very easy to trace through and pin to fabric: use scissors to cut around the pattern piece and trace any notches or darts before removing the paper. As an alternative, use Reynolds Freezer Paper, available in quilt stores and online. The wax finish adheres to fabric when pressed with a hot, dry iron, allowing template cutting without pins. It's much quicker and I think more accurate. Templates can be reused six to eight times before the stickiness is gone.

## 10. PATTERN WEIGHTS

Lots of my dressmaker friends use pattern weights to hold paper patterns in place while they cut around the pieces with a rotary cutter.

## 11. FABRIC-SAFE MARKING PENS/PENCILS

Whether you are marking darts, matching points, letterbox rectangles or quilting lines, you will need fabric-safe pens or pencils that will show up on a variety of fabrics. I like Frixion pens, the marks of which can be removed with heat, and chalk pencils in a variety of colours, which can be brushed away. There is no such thing as the perfect marking tool, so it's useful to have a selection to hand and always test that the marks can be completely removed on scrap fabrics before you commit!

## 12. SEAM ROLLER

Perfect for flattening seams when you cannot use heat – for example with vinyl or faux leather.

## 13. SMALL BOWLS

A selection of small dishes are perfect for rounding corners on bag flaps.

## 14. PINS

Use good-quality long, thin pins for bag-making. Clover flower head and Taylor Seville magic pins are my absolute favourites.

## 15. WONDER CLIPS/QUILTERS CLIPS

These small plastic clips are absolutely ideal when you want to hold multiple or very thick layers together, such as the final putting together of a bag and lining. Clips are also the perfect solution when working with fabrics that would be damaged by pins, such as faux leather and vinyl.

## 16. 505 QUILT-BASTING SPRAY

This is a temporary spray adhesive much used by quilters to hold layers together for quilting. Use to hold bag fabrics to waddings, foams and interfacing while you quilt them. Washing removes the adhesive if you need to, but it is fabric safe and can be left in

## 17. FABRIC-SAFE GLUE STICK

Very useful for gluing in a zip prior to sewing or to prepare English paper piecing patches for speedier sewing. Use one specifically designed for sewing or you run the risk of damaging your fabric or sewing machine.

## 18. STILETTO OR TAILOR'S AWL

A sharply pointed tool useful for piercing holes for KAM snaps and screws. Also rather useful to hold fabric as you're feeding it through the sewing machine.

## 19. POINT TURNERS/CHOPSTICKS

You can buy fancy strap-turning tools and point turners, but a simple wooden chopstick does the job rather well, and I find I usually have one nearby or in my sewing kit! Japanese chopsticks are my favourites to use for turning since they have a more pointed but still slightly rounded end.

## 20. GOOD-QUALITY IRON AND PRESSING SURFACE

A decent-quality, heavy steam iron is so useful for any sewing job. I also like to have a small travel iron for ironing inside bags once they are made and for smaller detailed jobs. My preference is for a wool pressing mat as the mat holds heat well and the very firm surface gives amazing results.

6
7
13
20
PATTERN WEIGHTS
10
Odif
505
Colle Temporaire pour tissu
Temporary Adhesive for fabric
Temporärer Kleber für Stoff
16
17
Odif
505
Colle Temporaire
Temporary Adhesive Glue Stick
36 g
18
Size 5/10
John James
Est. 1840
Sharps
Finest Quality Needles
John James
Est. 1840
Embroidery
5
19
UNIVERSAL
Machine Needles
Heavy Assortment
Hemline
3
SCHM

8
15
14
ROXANNE
SHARP-N-CAP PACK
1 Sharpener, 4 Pencil Caps, 4 Pencils
11
Sewline FABRIC PENCIL
Sewline
FABRIC PENCIL
Clean, clear lines, easily erased

# HARDWARE

Alongside fabric and interfacing, the holy trinity of bag-making is completed by hardware: the (usually) metal parts we add to a bag to make it more functional, practical and stylish.

The hardware on a handmade bag can elevate it to near stratospheric heights, and the choice has never been wider! Just like fabric and interfacings, you'll want to stash gorgeous bag hardware whenever you see it so you're always ready to sew your next beautiful creation.

You can buy hardware in a number of different metallic finishes: gold, rose gold, silver, antique bronze, gunmetal and rainbow metallic finishes. You can also find some hardware in plastic or resin finishes, including solid, patterned and, my personal favourite, tortoiseshell finishes. I also include bag handles and straps/locks in with my hardware. These are available in leather, PU (vegan leather) resin, plastic, bamboo and beaded versions.

Quality counts and makes a noticeable difference. Look for good-quality finishes and a decent weight of metal for your bag hardware. And remember, the hardware rarely wears out, so if you tire of a bag but still love the metalware, just cut the hardware off the bag and reuse it.

### 1. D RINGS

Shaped like a capital letter D, these rings are usually added to the body of the bag to which a removable shoulder strap or handles can be clipped via swivel clips. The curved edge, in conjunction with a swivel clip, means that the strap will always 'centre'. They can also be used with a swivel clip to provide a lock or bag closure. I most commonly use these rings in ½", 1" and 1½" versions.

### 2. RECTANGULAR RINGS

Usually rectangular, as the name suggests, but sometimes square, these rings are useful for attaching a permanent (non-removable) strap or handle.

### 3. STRAP SLIDERS

Rectangular or square and shaped like a buckle with either a fixed or movable centre bar, a strap slider allows a handle or shoulder strap length to be adjustable. I most commonly use 1" and 1½" versions, but smaller ones are available and useful to use with very narrow webbing.

### 4. LOBSTER/SWIVEL CLASPS

These clips or clasps have a square end that is fixed to the bag permanently with a fabric tab or webbing and a 'lobster claw'-style end which can be opened and attached to a D ring, usually on a bag or handle. These clips are also very useful when making a key saver (a long strip of folded and stitched fabric attached at one end to a swivel clasp and the other end anchored in a seam of the bag lining to allow keys to be attached for easy retrieval, even when the bag is full!).

### 5. KAM SNAPS

These are a great option for a quick closure for a flap, pocket top or small bag. The snap itself comes in two halves and each half has a corresponding pin or stud back that looks like a thumb tack or drawing pin. You'll need a fitting tool, which is often supplied in kit form with the snaps. Look for 'T5' – this is the size of KAM snaps I use.

### 6. SEW-ON PRESS STUDS

Available in a variety of sizes and metal finishes, sew-on press studs are usually attached after the bag is completed and are a good 'afterthought' to close a bag or pocket.

### 7. MAGNETIC SNAPS

A two-part magnetic closure that is a very popular choice for closing a bag, either on tabs inside the bag, on a flap or flap closure, or for 'pinching' in the sides of a bag. They are quick and easy to fit with no more than a small sharp pair of scissors. Available in a variety of metal finishes.

14
16
15
9
10
4
1
13
12
3
6
5
11
2
8

## 8. TONGUE LOCKS AND MAGNETIC SEW-ON BUCKLES

Both provide a very smart, very professional and high-end finish to even the simplest bag. Usually made of leather and metal, they come in two parts and are typically sewn to the flap and the body of a bag. The 'buckle' element is faux and the closure is essentially a fancy, visible magnetic snap masquerading as something far more complex. The tongue locks clip together with a very satisfying 'click' and look far more impressive than the minimal skills needed to fit them! Both require hand sewing to attach them.

## 9. TWIST LOCKS

A two-part lock that usually locks a bag flap to the body of the bag. A hole is made in the finished flap with a smart metal cover completely encapsulating the raw edges, and this is then covered at the back with a screw-on metal plate. A twisting metal knob is attached to the bag via prongs and a washer. They are a little more challenging to install than other locks but worth it for the va-va-voom!

## 10. SMALL SCREWDRIVER

I kept a small pack of screwdrivers from a Christmas cracker – I can't tell you how useful they've been over the years, particularly when it comes to fitting twist locks! Mini or 'precision' screwdriver sets are available online, or you could just wait for Christmas and keep your fingers crossed!

## 11. ZIPS

Zips are a fantastic addition to a bag. They look smart and give a professional polished look to your makes, but they also provide security for your belongings and can add a flash of colour just where you need it. Zips have had something of a makeover in recent years, and you can now find multicoloured teeth, different metallic finishes, fancy striped or patterned zipper tapes and a very wide choice of zips you can cut to length.

Don't be afraid of zips; they're not hard to sew into a bag and you can practise with scrap fabric and a spare zip until you are ready to use one in your bags. I always use nylon zips as they can be sewn over (with care) and cut to length with kitchen scissors. Look for regular/haberdashery zips rather than 'invisible' zips in the haberdashery department. These zips tend to be #3 (the narrowest zips I use in my bag-making and are good for smaller projects or inside pockets). If you can't find anything else, you can use #3 zips for all the projects in this book that require a zip.

I also use a lot of #5 zips in bag-making. They are chunkier and wider than a #3 and make more of an impact, so I often use them for the outside of a bag. Many 'zip-on-a-roll' options are available, and most, but not all, come with a number of attached zipper pulls. Check before you buy, and if your zipper doesn't have pulls attached you'll need to buy some in the corresponding size.

## 12. ZIP PULLS

Lift the look of a zip you already have, add to a zip to make a double zipper or use with 'zip on a roll'! There are lots of fantastic, fun and fancy zipper pulls to add an extra bit of bling to your bags. Keep in mind that #5 zips need #5 pulls. If you're using standard haberdashery zippers, these are #3 and require the corresponding size of zipper pull.

## 13. ZIP JIG

While not essential, this handy tool makes the job of putting the zip pull onto a zip tape quick and easy. I wouldn't be without mine!

## 14. SEW-ON BAG HANDLES

Usually made of PU/faux leather and sometimes real leather (always check the product information). They come in a wide assortment of fashion and classic colours. The ones I use are typically around 24" long and are usually sold in pairs. The sewing holes are already punched so you just use a regular hand-sewing needle and strong thread to backstitch them to your bag. Occasionally I'll use ready-made handles that end with a ring; these are designed to be attached with fabric loops/tabs and need to be incorporated into your bag as you are making it.

## 15. PLASTIC AND RESIN HANDLES

I love circular plastic or resin handles for knitting-style bags, but you can also use square or trapezoid versions to similar effect. An internal aperture of around 5" is ideal for most applications. A pair of plastic or resin handles can also be added instead of short shoulder straps/handles – just make a wide tab/loop that just fits the internal dimensions and use this to attach the handle to the top of the bag prior to insertion of the lining.

## 16. CLIP-ON SHOULDER STRAPS

I love making my own shoulder straps, but sometimes I want a different look or a quicker finish. I love using detachable ready-made shoulder straps. I'll often make a fabric strap and have a ready-made one to swap out to give my bag a really different look. Just add D rings to either side of your chosen bag instead of a sewn-in handle. Then make your shoulder strap (or buy it) with lobster/swivel clasps attached and you will be able to mix and match your bags and straps. A few accessories can really switch up the look of your bag!

brother

# TECHNIQUES

## USING 'EASY' FABRICS

Most of the bags in this book are made with 100 per cent cotton fabrics – the kind you find in a quilt store. Quilt-weight cotton is super easy to work with, comes in an almost endless array of designs and colours, and presses and washes really well. I mean, really, what's not to love? I'm all about making life easy, so I tend to avoid fabrics with stretch or ones that are terribly thick and would make for a bulky and difficult project.

Making your own bags is a brilliant way to express your personality, so feel free to completely ignore the fabric choices I've made in favour of something that speaks to you and is about you! Making your own is the key to making bags that are perfect. I'm not talking exam perfection here, I'm talking about the perfect style, colour, theme or use for you!

One piece of advice I do want to share, though, is if you're going to use directional fabrics (stripes, plaids or checks), think carefully about how you will cut them out before you reach for your scissors. I love to use bold or subtle directional prints as they add a lot of bang for your buck, but I often restrict them to bag fronts, pockets or flaps: the pieces are large and show off the prints well, but I don't have the headache of matching patterns across numerous seams and it makes the print a real focal point ... easy impact without any hassle!

You can pre-wash your washable fabrics before you begin if you wish; I don't and I've never had a problem. One thing I always do is to give my fabrics a good press before I start cutting out. Steam press if you can as it'll tighten the fabric up and mean that any shrinkage in the fabric is likely to happen before you cut your pattern pieces, which is what you want.

## USING TRICKY FABRICS

If you're using quilt-weight cottons, cotton canvas or denim to make a bag, it's all plain sailing. Fabrics such as these are very stable and easy to cut and press. They behave themselves when they're being sewn and offer up no challenges for even a novice sewer.

Sometimes, though, you might be tempted to used 'tricky' fabrics – those with special properties/coatings or finishes that just require a little extra 'management'. These fabrics are most definitely to be embraced; for many they are bag-making staples! I'm talking about vinyl, oil cloth, tapestry, faux leather and cork.

**My top tips for working with tricky fabrics**

1. They tend to be thicker, so cut only one layer at a time.
2. A lot of tricky fabrics are also difficult or impossible to iron. Use a seam roller to flatten seams, and if your vinyl or faux leather is creased, use a hot iron to warm up your ironing board and then lay your fabric onto the warmed surface and place a heavy book or tailor's clapper onto the fabric and allow it to cool.
3. Most are difficult or impossible to pin. Use quilters clips to hold thick layers together and to avoid holes in your fabrics. Use low-tack masking tape or double-sided sew-in tape to hold zips in place as you sew.
4. If fabric is fraying badly (particularly tapestry), overlock or zigzag the edges of the fabric pieces before you sew them together.
5. Use a walking foot for sewing thick layers and invest in a non-stick or 'Teflon' foot for sewing 'sticky' fabrics like faux leather, oil cloth and vinyl.
6. Use a slightly longer stitch for construction and also for topstitching.
7. Take it slow and check before you sew! You don't really want to unpick, ever, but particularly with fabrics that don't 'heal' and will leave telltale holes.
8. Make an 'easy-fabric' version first, just to get the hang of things.

## CUTTING OUT USING A ROTARY CUTTER OR A PAPER PATTERN

The vast majority of the pattern pieces in this book are rotary cut and are based on strips and large squares or rectangles. If you're not sure about rotary cutting, then read on as I cover this in this chapter.

If you'd rather go old-school and use scissors, that will work perfectly too – just measure and mark out the shapes on your fabric with tailor's chalk or a marking pen, then cut the pieces out with dressmaking scissors.

If a pattern calls for a paper pattern, just trace the pattern piece onto dressmakers tissue paper, which you've ironed first to remove any wrinkles.

Rough-cut the paper pattern and pin it to the fabric, or use pattern weights, then cut out pattern pieces and fabrics in one go, following the outer line.

You might need to add notches to your fabric pieces (these are marked with a little triangle and are usually used to help line up or match pieces that need to fit together): snip a triangle into the seam allowance at this point.

To mark a dart, poke a pin through the tip of the dart and then mark with a fabric-safe pen. Mark the wide points of the dart with a dot too, then join the wide points up to the tip with your fabric-safe pen. All seam allowances are included, unless otherwise stated.

Most of the pattern pieces need to be cut out with straight sides on the 'straight of grain', parallel to the selvedge on your fabric. If you're using a printed fabric you'd naturally do it this anyway, so that the patterns on your fabric are the right way up and 'straight'. Cutting pattern pieces on the straight of grain ensures that the edges stay straight and don't stretch out of shape when you're sewing, since the lengthways and crossways grainlines are most stable. Where possible, cut shoulder straps on the lengthways grain (running north to south along the selvedge) as this is the most stable grainline and there is little or no stretch.

## CUTTING FABRIC 'ON THE BIAS'

Sometimes we need to embrace fabric's weird ability to stretch. There's very little stretch in the lengthways or crossways grains of woven fabric, but cut fabric at a 45-degree angle and the picture is very different! Cutting through the warp and weft means that the edges of the fabric stretch quite a bit, and this is brilliant when you need to sew a binding around a curved edge.

Line up the 45-degree mark on your rotary ruler with a straight edge on the fabric – the cutting edge of the ruler will be positioned across the fabric at a 45-degree angle. Simply cut along the ruler's edge and then cut the binding strips from that edge. Watch how you handle fabrics cut on the bias: be gentle with them or they will stretch out of shape and the edges will go frilly – not the look we are going for!

## 'FUSSY CUTTING' FABRIC

Sometimes you'll find a fabric with a motif, print or weave that you really want to make a feature of, and when you do, that's called 'fussy cutting'. It might be a big bloom, perfectly centred on a bag flap, or a pocket that matches up with the fabric of the main bag without interrupting the pattern on the fabric. Fussy cutting is when you make sure the strip on a fabric is straight when cut, or you might choose to cut a plaid on the bias to create a different look on the pockets or gusset.

To fussy cut a motif centrally, simply divide the width of the fabric piece being cut by two and find the centre point of the important motif. Measure out the half width from this point, and cut. Do the same from the centre out to the other side.

Repeat this step for the length of the piece. If you're using a template, just find the centre of the pattern piece and mark a cross. Find the centre of the motif and match up the two points.

## SIMPLE PIECING/SEAM ALLOWANCES

Seam allowances vary depending on the project. Most projects and seam allowances are ¼", but check the pattern before you proceed. To make a simple seam, place the two fabrics right sides together and match the raw edges. Pin the fabrics together carefully (I like to pin at the start and end of the seam first, then any important match points or notches, and then I pin in between these points).

Always remove pins before you get to them on the sewing machine – never sew over pins! Once your seams are sewn, set them with a warm iron and then press the seam to one side or open.

## SEWING HEAVY LAYERS

When bag-making, we often have to sew quite thick or heavy layers, particularly in the latter stages of making a bag. There are a few things you can do to make this easier:

- Use a suitable needle. I like size 90 or 100 for bag-making. These needles are a bit thicker than the sort I'd use for piecing and go through thick layers much easier.
- Hold layers together with quilters clips rather than pins – clips handle the heavy layers with ease.
- Use a slightly longer stitch length on your sewing machine.
- Sew more slowly.
- Use a walking foot to feed the fabrics evenly and prevent creeping layers, tucks and folds.
- Trim away bulky interfacing, foam and fabric from seam allowances if you are able to.

## ADDING STRUCTURE TO A BAG WITH INTERFACING, FUSIBLE FLEECE AND FUSIBLE FOAM

A lot of the bags in this book have a layer of 'interfacing' added to make the fabric firmer. Most often I will use interfacing on the linings and pockets to make them sturdier and more structured, but sometimes I use it for an outer bag when I want a thinner, less bulky bag. I like to use medium-weight fusible interfacing, which you iron onto the wrong side of your chosen fabric. Whichever interfacing you use will come with instructions for fusing, usually printed on the edge of the interfacing. Use the correct heat: I like medium/two spot and steam, or I'll cover the interfacing with a damp cloth. Take your time when you're ironing interfacing as the 'bond' isn't instant; it'll take up to 15 seconds of continuous heat to do that, but don't take my word for it – follow the manufacturer's instructions!

Fusible fleece is another great option for adding soft structure and a little padding or relief when quilting. I like H640 and H630 (a little thinner) when I want a thin bag but still want to show off my quilting.

I use fusible foam when I want a padded bag with a really great firm structure. These bags will literally stand up by themselves but are still soft and easy to sew. My preference is for Bosal In-R-Form foam or Vlieseline Style-Vil.

I like to cut all interfacings, fleeces and foams ¼" or more smaller on all sides than the piece of fabric I'm sticking it to. That means that the fabric in the seam allowances isn't 'bulked out' with an extra couple of layers. It takes a little longer to cut out and you'll have to cut fabrics and interfacing separately, but I think it's worth the extra step. Experiment with interfacing; even quilt-weight cottons vary in thickness and firmness. Try different weights of interfacing until you get the level of firmness that suits your project.

## ADDING SEWN DARTS

Darts can be added to a bag to create extra fullness, shape and internal space. They are a staple of dressmaking and are really easy to sew. Darts will be shown on a paper pattern (they look like long slim triangles pointing into the bag).

Mark the dart onto the wrong side of the fabric piece, then fold the fabric at the dart matching the wide points. Sew on the line that joins the outer point with the inner point. Press the dart one way. Be a little careful when you are pressing the bag as you've created a fuller shape with the dart, so don't then undo your good work by pressing the whole thing flat. Use a tailor's ham or a small rolled-up towel inside the bag to keep the shape while you press the bag.

## SEWING IN A GUSSET

Some bags have a three-part gusset. These make a 'box' bag. Others have a continuous gusset that creates a more smoothly curving shape to the bag. Once you've cut out the gusset and fused/quilted if necessary, you need to find the centre and mark it with a pin.

Do the same with the bag front, then bring the centre point of the bag front and gusset, right sides together, and pin. Now use lots of pins to attach the gusset to the bag front. I usually add a little wiggle room/length to the gusset, so just keep pinning until you get to the top of the bag and repeat out from the centre of the gusset to the other side of the bag.

You might need to notch the seam allowance to help you get around the curves. Sew in place, then repeat the process on the bag back. Trim the top of the gusset if you need to.

When sewing in a continuous gusset there isn't really any wiggle room, but if it seems a little too long you can always make a small tuck in the centre bottom where it won't be seen.

## ADDING APPLIQUÉ

You can add appliqués to your bags quickly and easily to create fun 'patches' or to add decorative and strengthening 'corners' on bags.

1 Mark out your chosen appliqué onto the non-fusible side of a piece of fusible medium-weight interfacing. Pin this interfacing to the right side of the appliqué fabric, with the fusible side touching the right side of the fabric, then sew on the drawn line.

2 Trim the fabric and interfacing to within ⅛" of the sewn line. Cut a small slash in the centre of the interfacing, then turn the appliqué through to the right side. Finger press the turned edge.

3 Now place the appliqué, fusible-side down, onto the right side of your bag piece and fuse in place with a dry iron. Topstitch or blanket stitch around the appliqué to attach it to the bag.

## QUILTING

Most bags consist of three layers: an outer, a lining and some kind of interfacing or padding in the middle. The construction stitches are generally enough to keep these layers together, but for extra style and a more beautiful aesthetic I like to add quilting. This means simply stitching through all three layers (or often just the outer and padding) to add extra pattern and dimension but also to make the fabric of the bag more cohesive and strong.

Many of the interfacings/fleeces and foams that I use are fusible, but if not I use 505 quilt-basting spray to temporarily hold the layers together while I do the quilting.

I quilt a lot of my bags with crosshatching: to do this you'll need a fabric-safe marking pen and a ruler. I use the straight edge of the fabric as a guide to mark lines at a 45-degree angle in one direction and then the other, spacing my lines at between 1" and 2", depending on the scale of the bag. Sometimes I don't bother with the true 45-degree line and just mark my first lines from corner to corner and then space the lines out from these foundations. Other times I will use the width of the sewing machine foot as my guide to space out straight lines of quilting.

Use a walking foot on your machine to feed the thick layers evenly and avoid wrinkles. Increase your stitch length to a 3.0 or 3.5 and do a couple of reverse stitches at the start and finish of your quilting, hidden in the seam allowance. Remove your pen/pencil lines once the quilting is completed.

## TOPSTITCHING

Topstitching serves a couple of very important roles in bag-making. It is used to hold things in place (often the edge of a bag), it keeps the lining in place and prevents it shifting, it's used around zips to attach them, or it's used to visibly hold a pocket, tab or strap in place. We also use topstitching to add a neat and decorative finish to a bag or to add importance to an area of a bag. So all in all, it's usually very visible and it's worth taking your time over.

Use a slightly longer stitch, perhaps a 3.0 (some makers like to use a slightly thicker thread for topstitching so it's more prominent), or use a decorative thread like a variegated, metallic or highly contrasting colour. Topstitching looks best when it's approximately ⅛" to ¼" away from the edge of the fabric.

## PIPING SEAMS/EDGES

Piped seams are a very high-end added touch to a bag. They are completely optional but rather lovely done in a contrasting colour. Piping looks particularly good around a front flap on a messenger bag or around the front and back panels to frame them. You'll need some thin piping cord (I like to use 3mm).

1 Measure the length of the sides you wish to pipe and add 5" to the length. Cut fabric strips on the bias at approximately 2" wide and join with diagonal seams to make a piece long enough to cover the cord. Lay the cord onto the wrong side of the fabric strip and fold the fabric over the cord, bringing the long raw edges of the fabric together.

2 Now use the zipper foot on your sewing machine to sew close to the cord, all along the fabric strip. Trim the fabric strip back to ⅜", then pin or tack the covered piping cord around the three sides of the bag flap (you might need to snip into the fabric to turn corners). The flap should be at the construction stage, layered with batting or foam and quilted only. Make sure the raw edge of the piping cord lines up with the raw edge of the flap.

3 Add the lining fabric over the top of the flap and piping cord, right sides together, and pin in place. Now sew around the three sides of the flap using the zipper foot again and getting as close as possible to the piping cord. Turn the flap through to the right side and press.

To add piping to the front/back panels of a bag, simply baste the covered cord to the sides and bottom edge of the front and back pieces, then make up the bag as normal. You will still need to use the zipper foot to get close enough to the cord, so it's worth marking the required seam allowance before you attach the cord.

## ZIPS

Putting zips into bags is a natural fit! Zips keep things secure, and keep the contents of your bag safe. Zips cause many sewers a flutter of nerves, but there's absolutely no need to feel anxious as zips are actually easy to master! Buy a 10" or 12" zip, grab some scrap fabrics and practise a few times at least before you tackle the same job in one of your bags.

My absolute favourite zips for bags are number 5 (often referred to as #5) zips. They are chunky and gorgeous, and the tape or teeth come in a whole host of fancy colours! Look for ones with nylon teeth as these are easy to cut to length and sew over (carefully!). #5 zip is often sold in long lengths with numerous zip pulls attached. I also buy smart or quirky zipper pulls to add to my bags for an extra flourish. Don't forget to match the size: #5 zip pulls for #5 zip tape, and invest in a zip jig to make putting on the pulls a much easier task.

### SHORTENING ZIPS

Sometimes you have the perfect zip: the colour and style are great, but it's too long. Not a problem!

1 Measure the length you need from the top of the zip pull down towards the stop and mark a line with pencil.

2 Use your sewing machine and a straight stitch to sew across your marked line three or four times to create a new stop. Trim the excess zip away, leaving about ½" 'allowance'. It's a great idea to do this line of stitching at the top end too: just pull the zipper pull down out of the way, bring the ends of the zip back together, and stitch back and forth a few times. This ensures that when you insert the zip and need to open it, the ends won't splay open!

### MAKING ZIP ENDS →

Zip ends add a really professional touch to a zip and help it to blend or stand out from the rest of the bag. Zip ends can also be used to make a zip just a little longer, meaning a 9" zip really will fit a 10" bag top!

1 Cut two strips of fabric the width of your zip (most often 1–1½" and 5" in length). Press a ¼" in at both short ends to neaten.

2 Fold the strip in half, wrong sides together, and press. Slip one end of the zip into the neatened ends so that the ¼" seam allowance covers about ½" of the zip tape, then carefully topstitch through all layers. Snip through the fold and trim away the extra zip from the seam allowance.

Repeat the process at the other end of the zip. Trim the neatened zip to the required length, keeping the amount of 'zip end' equal at both ends.

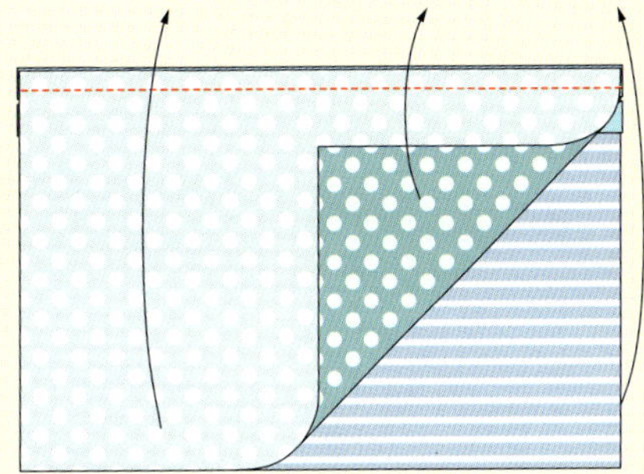

**SEWING A SIMPLE ZIP →**

These are your 'bread-and-butter' zips, and are perfect for adding a zip to the top of a pouch bag or a zip on the back or front of a plain bag.

1 Cut two pieces of fabric for the top of the zip: one outer and one lining, the same size as each other. Do the same for the bottom of the zip. Most of the time, this 'top and bottom' will actually be the front and back of the bag.

2 Sandwich one side of the zip between the outer and lining fabrics for the top. Using the zipper foot on your sewing machine to sew along the raw edges, sew a scant ¼".

3 Open the lining and outer fabrics up and press them back away from the zip, then fold them back on themselves so that the wrong sides are touching. Match the side and bottom edges of the outer and lining carefully and press, then topstitch very close to the zip, again using the zipper foot. Repeat this process on the other side of the zip.

If you're nervous about sewing the outer and lining in one step, you can always sew the outer to the zip first, then add the lining. Sew a tiny bit further in than the first line of stitching to make sure you don't see those stitches!

## MAKING A 'LETTERBOX' ZIP →

A letterbox zip is a sleek and professional-looking closure to a pocket and has the advantage of being part of the 'body' of the bag. It can be used on the inside or outside of a bag.

1 Cut two rectangles of fabric for the lining of the pocket, both the same size. On the wrong side of one of the rectangles, draw a rectangular 'letterbox', which is usually the length of your zip by ½" wide.

2 Position this marked fabric piece right-side down onto the right side of your bag panel in the specified position. Sew around the letterbox, making sure that you sew right on your drawn lines and pivoting at each of the four corners. I like to use a shorter stitch than normal: 1.8–2.0 in length.

3 Carefully cut down the centre of the letterbox and also snip into the corners. Cut to the line of stitching but not through it!

4 Turn the rectangle of fabric through the letterbox and press the edges really crisply and neatly. I like to do this with my fingers first, get a great finish and then use my iron to press everything flat.

5 Baste the zip behind the letterbox so that the right side of the zip is showing on the right side of the back. I like to hand baste (tack) the zip in place, then sew around the zip from the right side using the sewing machine and the zipper foot.

6 Working from the wrong side, pin the other rectangle of lining fabric to the first, being sure to keep the pocket linings away from the body of the bag. Sew around the edges of the pinned rectangles to join them together. Continue making the bag.

## BINDING EDGES

Bindings are used to add a decorative edging to pockets and the tops of some bags. They can also be used to finish the edges of a quilted project. There are two different binding methods you might find useful. I always neaten one short end of my binding by folding in ½" and pressing, then I'll simply slip the other raw end of the binding under this fold to neaten the ends.

### SINGLE-FOLD BINDING

1 Start by cutting strips of fabric that are 1¼" wide by the length you need (I always cut extra length to make the binding strip easier to handle). Fold and press the strip in half, wrong sides together, unfold the binding and then turn a ¼" hem on the other long raw edge and press.

2 Lay the binding on the edge to be bound, working from the outside of your bag or pocket, right sides together and raw edges aligned. Sew a ¼" seam allowance to attach the binding to the bag, fold the binding up and over the raw edge to cover it, bringing the other neatened edge down over the back of your work. It should sit slightly lower than the first line of stitching, thereby covering it.

3 Pin the binding in place, then sew the binding to the back of your work by hand. Alternatively, topstitch from the front, sewing very close to the bottom edge of the binding to catch the binding at the back. Single-fold binding is great to use on areas of medium-to-light use and also uses half as much fabric as double-fold binding, so if fabric is in short supply use this method.

### DOUBLE-FOLD BINDING

1 Start with a binding strip that is 2½" wide by the required length – again, I always cut extra length. Fold the strip in half lengthways, wrong sides together. Align the two raw edges of the binding to the raw edge of your bag, pocket or quilt and sew a ¼" seam allowance.

2 Turn the folded fabric up and over the raw edge and slip-stitch the binding to the back of your work. Double-fold binding is a thicker, more robust binding and is perfect for edges that will suffer very heavy wear and tear.

## LINING A BAG

The lining of a bag is just as important as the outer bag; you could argue that it is used more, so it's worth getting the lining right. Give it some love and use a beautiful fabric for the lining. I prefer something fairly light and bright and plain-ish, as I want to be able to see what's in my bag easily. I like to interface the linings of most bags with medium-weight fusible interfacing. I also treat any internal pockets in the same way. I've kept most of the linings pretty simple – add slip or letterbox zippered pockets as you wish. Customise your linings in the same way you would the outer bag.

### ADDING A SIMPLE LINING TO A BAG

Most of the time I make a separate lining, usually made in exactly the same way as the outer bag but with a gap in one of the seams. I leave a gap that is four fingers wide – if I can get four fingers through the gap it will be big enough to turn pretty much anything through. If your bag is very stiff, large or has large handles attached, you can make the gap wider.

The outer bag is then placed inside the lining, right sides together, and the top edge seam is sewn, joining the outer and lining together. The bag is turned through the gap, and once I've checked the top seam to make sure everything is looking good, I can close the gap in the lining, either by hand with small invisible slip stitches or by machine, simply bringing the neatened edges of the gap together and sewing very close to the edge.

### MAKING A 'DROP-IN' LINING

Sometimes the lining can be 'dropped inside' a bag, wrong side to wrong side, and then the edges just need to be bound. This is also how a quilt or quilted bag is often finished. Refer to binding techniques (left) for how to do this.

## MAKING STRAPS/RING LOOPS AND HANDLES

Most of the bags in this book have a shoulder strap or handles of some kind, and often there are 'tabs' holding metalware in place, like D or O rings and swivel clips. I use two methods for making mine.

### MAKING NARROW STRAPS AND TABS

For a narrow strap or tab, cut a strip of fabric and then press it in half lengthways, wrong sides together. Open out the fold and then turn the long raw edges in to meet the centre crease. Press again. Finally, fold the strip in half down the original centre fold to enclose the outer raw edges. Topstitch carefully down both of the long sides.

If you need the short ends neatened too, then turn and press a ½" hem on the strip as step one, then follow the instructions above.

This is also the method I use when making any size strap from faux leather. The fabric is much too thick to turn through a tube, so I use this folded method. You'll need to cut the strap double the finished width required plus ½". So for a 1½" wide strap, cut a strip of faux leather 3½" wide. You do not need to cut lining since the strap will be faux leather on both sides. Run a line of ¼" wide double-sided sewable tape down each of the long edges. Turn a ¼" hem in on each side onto the double-sided tape.

Now run another line of ¼" tape down one long edge and fold the strap in half onto this tape. Finally, topstitch down both long edges to finish the strap.

### MAKING WIDER STRAPS AND TABS

1 For wider straps and for tabs, cut two strips of fabric (you might well like to interface the outer fabric with interfacing or Waist-Shaper for a stiffer, firmer finish). Make sure there is no interfacing in your seam allowance. Place the two strips of fabric, right sides together, and sew both long edges and one short edge, leaving one narrow end unsewn.

2 At the short-sewn end, make a deep indentation with your thumb and then push a chopstick into this hollow. Rest the end of the chopstick on a table and pull the strap down onto the chopstick until the short-sewn end is pushed right through the open end. Grab the neater end and pull the whole strap through to the right side.

3 Press the shoulder strap carefully, then topstitch the long edges very close to the seams. Cut this down to make shorter lengths if required.

### MAKING HANDLES

You can make quick and easy handles for your bags using the same method as making shoulder straps. Make a little over double the length of each handle (so enough for two handles, plus a little extra), then cut your handle lengths from this strap.

Measure approximately 3" in from each end of the strap and place a mark. Fold the handle, wrong sides together, and pin the centre section between the marks. Topstitch through all layers between these marks to create a double-thickness handle. Pin the flat, wider ends to your bag and baste in place, then add the lining.

## SEWING A 'CROSS' FOR STRENGTH

Use this technique when you are attaching straps to bags or when finishing the ends of an adjustable strap slider for a very strong and durable join. You're going to sew a box with a cross through the middle: you can mark this with an erasable marker if you wish, or eyeball it!

1 Start by bringing the bobbin thread to the top and hold both top and bobbin threads as you start stitching (this is to prevent a 'bird's nest' forming on the back of your work). Stitch forward and back a couple of times to secure the thread, then sew the outside 'box'.

2 Once you get back to the start, sew diagonally through the middle to the opposite corner, sew the bottom of the box for a second time, then sew to the opposite corner. Finally, sew back across the top and reverse a couple of stitches to secure.

## ADDING AN ADJUSTABLE STRAP SLIDER →

This is the perfect addition to any shoulder strap where you need the length to be adjustable; a cross-body messenger bag is a great example. Most of the time I wear mine across my body, but occasionally I need the strap to be shorter so I can wear it on my shoulder. Strap sliders look like a buckle and are fitted in quite a similar way.

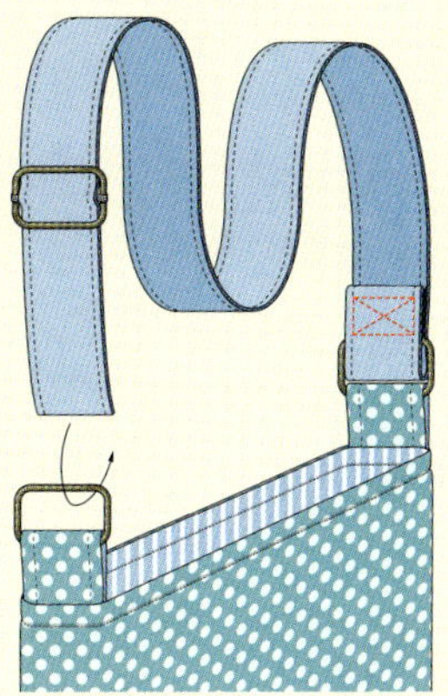

1 Attach one end of the shoulder strap to the bag as normal – just thread it through the rectangular ring, overlap the end of the strap and sew with a 'cross'. Now thread the strap slider onto the strap and slide it about halfway along the strap. Poke the unattached end of the strap through the other rectangular ring and then form the shoulder strap into a 'ring', doubling the strap back on itself.

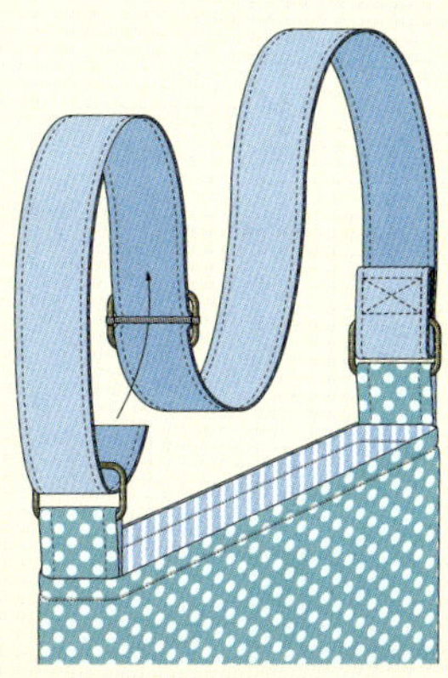

2 Pass the unattached end through the back of the strap slider, passing it over the centre bar. Bring the end of the strap back onto the strap, matching lining side to lining side. This should be about 4" away from the strap slider. Pin in place, then sew a 'cross' (see opposite) to attach the strap.

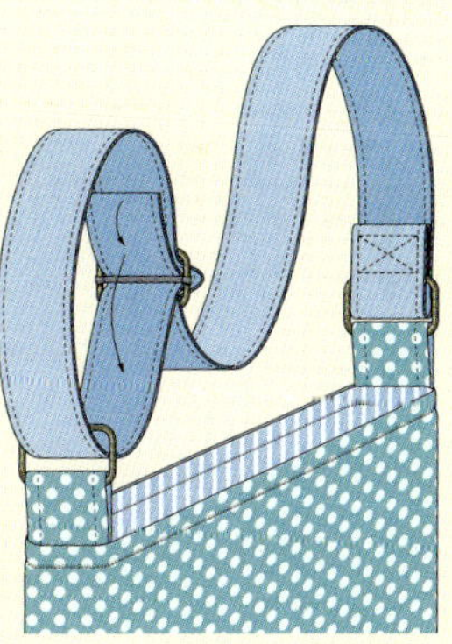

## MAKING WEBBING STRAPS AND HANDLES

I love using cotton or nylon webbing to make bag straps and handles. It's very durable and smart looking, creates almost instant straps and handles, and there are lots of plain and fancy varieties available in an assortment of widths.

If you're using the nylon version, use a lighter to melt the cut ends to seal them. You really only have to show the flame to the webbing for a brief second to seal it. Take care doing this; it really is the merest wave of the lighter flame.

To create a really cohesive look, add neat strips of coordinating fabric, topstitched to the webbing. To do this, cut a length of fabric to the same length as the webbing and also the same width. Neatly fold and press a narrow ¼" hem down both long edges of the fabric, then centre it onto the webbing so that a ¼" of the webbing is showing on either side. Hold the fabric in place with quilters clips, then topstitch the fabric neatly in place on both edges.

## ADDING 'SEW-ON' HANDLES

I use a lot of ready-made, sew-on handles. They lend such a professional look to bags and are very widely available in a great range of colours. They are usually made of PU or faux leather and have the stitching holes already punched through them, making them a breeze to hand sew to the finished bag. I like to use a tiny dab of strong glue on the back of the handle, right in the middle of where you will sew but nowhere near the actual sewing holes.

Place the handle into position onto the finished bag and hold in place with quilters clips, or place a heavy book on top until the glue has dried.

Next, use a length of extra-strong polyester or linen thread in a matching colour to hand sew the handles in place. Use a backstitch through all layers and at the end of the line of stitches go over the first couple of stitches to reinforce. Take the thread through to the lining side of the bag and finish it off neatly.

## USING LOBSTER/SWIVEL CLASPS

Lobster or swivel clasps are such a useful piece of hardware for the bag maker. These are generally used to make something removable, like a shoulder strap or handles, but they can also be used to attach a bag to your belt loops, or to attach keys. They can even be used to close/lock a bag flap. Lobster/swivel clasps are generally used in conjunction with a D ring, which the clasp clips into. The D ring can be any size usually, since the swivel clasp only needs to be able to clip on, so I tend to use the smaller D rings for this job.

## MAKING A FASTENING FLAP OR BAG FLAP

Some of the bags in this book have a flap that closes the main compartment of the bag completely, while others have a narrower gap that still closes the bag but just in the middle. Both are made and applied in the same way and are easy to add to an open-style bag if you prefer something more secure.

Cut out the outer flap, the inner flap/lining and the interfacing or foam. Layer the outer flap with wadding or interfacing and quilt as desired. If you are using a magnetic snap, apply it to the flap lining.

Layer the quilted outer flap with the lining piece and sew around the sides and bottom, leaving the top open. Turn through to the right side, then press and topstitch the three sewn sides.

## ADDING A 'TWIST LOCK' ↓

A twist lock is a very stylish addition to a flap closure. It's a little trickier to apply, so practise first on a mock-up of the flap. The twist lock comes in two parts: the smaller 'twist' part is attached to the main back via two prongs that go through the main bag prior to lining. A washer is added, just like adding a magnetic snap. The other part, the 'hole', is applied to the flap.

You'll need a small screwdriver to open up the back of this section. Use the back plate to mark the position of the hole and the screw holes. Cut the hole out of the flap and make some holes for the screws to pass through. Place the front part over the hole and push through, then place the back plate on and put the screws back in.

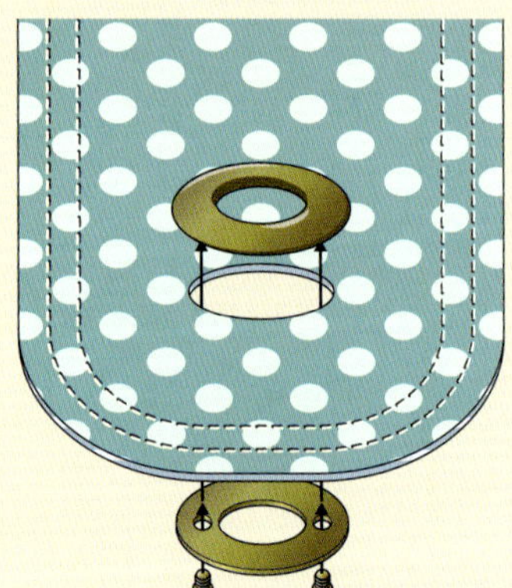

## ADDING A 'SEW-ON' TONGUE LOCK OR MAGNETIC BUCKLE

If you want to add a really professional clasp or lock to your bags with flaps, then have a look for tongue locks or magnetic buckles. They are usually made of real leather for durability, although synthetics are sometimes available. Both versions come in two pieces: the main buckle or tongue lock goes onto the flap, and the smaller part is stitched onto the main body of the bag.

I like to place the main part on the flap first: glue and stitch first as with sew-on handles. Next, attach the other half to the main lock and use this to centre and place in the best position. Mark the main bag position, then uncouple the lock and sew the smaller part to the main bag. Use a backstitch and strong polyester or linen thread to do this.

## ADDING A PRESS STUD FASTENING

Sew-on press studs are a fantastic first step to adding locks and fastenings to a bag since they can be added after the bag is completed and just require a needle and thread.

Mark the position of both halves on your bag or pocket, then sew the snap on with double thread and small overcasting stitches.

## ADDING MAGNETIC SNAPS ↓

Magnetic snaps are a great way to create a secure fastening for a bag, but they can also be used to 'clip in' the sides of a wide bag to change the profile. Magnetic snaps come in two halves, with prongs on the back, and have a washer each. They are fitted as the bag is being constructed, before the lining is added.

Mark the position of the snap on your bag and then use the washer to draw two lines/slots. Cut through the slots to make way for the prongs, push the prongs through the holes, then slip the washer over the back. Open the prongs out to secure the magnetic snap in place.

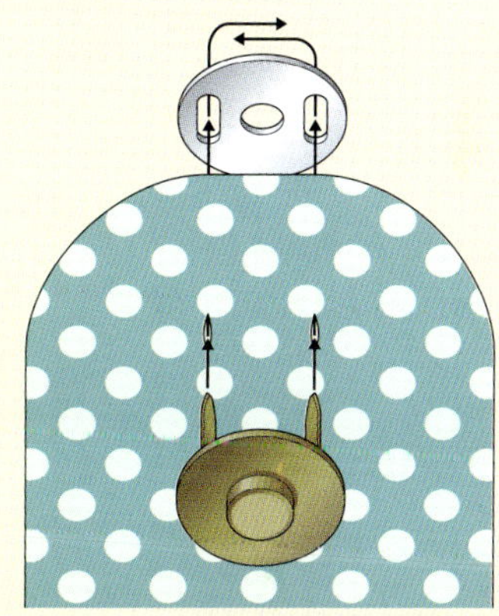

## ATTACHING A PRESS STUD OR KAM SNAP

KAM snaps or press studs can be attached to bag flaps or pocket tops very easily and are a quick, professional way to close an opening. You can buy boxes of snaps in a wide variety of colours (look for size T5). You'll also need a fitting tool, which looks like a fancy set of pliers. The snaps have a male and female half and both halves need a 'backing stud', which looks like a thumb tack or drawing pin. They are often sold together in kits.

Mark the position of the snap, then make a hole through the flap or bag using a thin, sharp tool or thick darning needle. Push the backing stud through the hole and place one half of the KAM snap over it. Crush the two together using the fitting tool. Repeat with the other half of the KAM snap.

## BOXING CORNERS →

This is a brilliant technique for adding depth and shape to a bag, which is essentially two flat rectangles sewn together.

Sew the side and base seams first, just as if you were making a flat tote. Use a ruler to mark a square at each of the bottom corners. The size will be given in the pattern, but generally this will be 1" to 3". Cut the square away using sharp scissors.

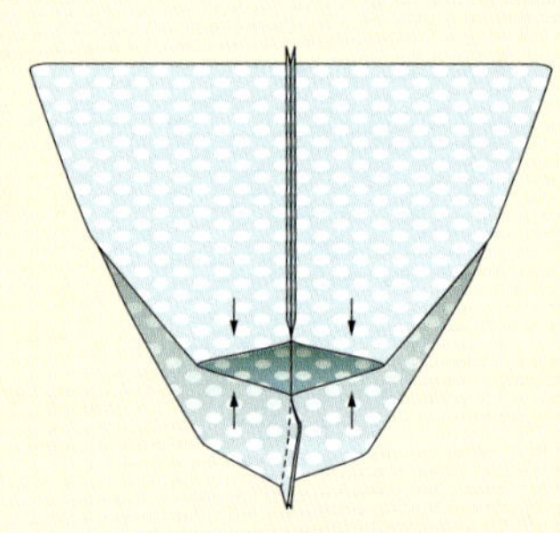

Bring the side and base seams together on one of the corners, bringing the cut edges together into a straight line. Sew this seam. Repeat on the other corner and you're done! Occasionally, a pattern might instruct you to cut the corners away first and then sew the side and base seams. If you're doing this, just remember to leave the sides of the square unsewn!

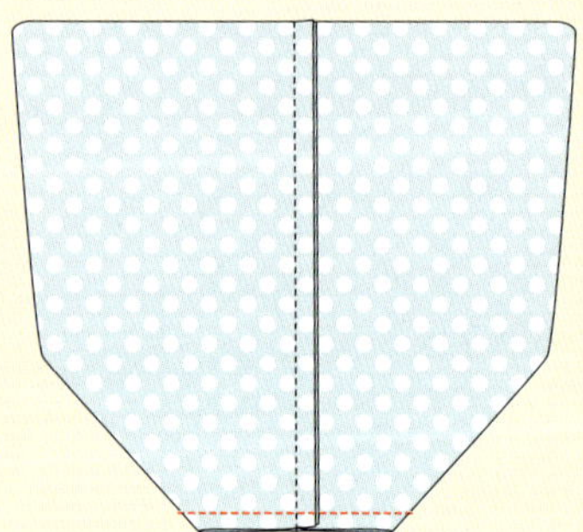

## MAKING A 'BOX' BAG

A 'box' bag has a front and a back and then three separate pieces to create a gusset. I prefer to use three separate pieces for this most of the time as it is really easy to achieve perfect corners. This is my favourite shape to use for bags, as it doesn't require pattern pieces. It can be simply rotary cut and the smart corners are really easy to achieve with my tips and techniques.

1 Set your pieces out into a 'net', then sew the front panel to the base panel. Start and finish your ¼" seam allowance ¼" in from each end and backstitch to secure. Sew the front of the back to the base panel in exactly the same way.

2 Sew the side panels to the back bag, starting sewing right at the very top of the bag and sewing down to ¼" from the bottom, backstitching as before. Repeat this on all four side seams.

3 Finally, sew the bottom side seams, starting and finishing the seams ¼" in from the ends and backstitching to secure.

You don't have to guess where ¼" from the end is! Measure and mark a pencil dot to show you where to start and finish.

## SEWING A BASIC 'SLIP' POCKET AND ONE WITH 'FAUX BINDING'

A 'slip' pocket is one that is completely flat and can either be inserted into a seam, usually in the lining, or can 'float' on another piece. A slip pocket is made by sewing two pieces of fabric together of equal size, one for the outer and one for the lining. Once the top seam has been sewn and the seam allowances pressed open, the fabrics are opened out and the lining and outer fabrics placed wrong sides together with the top seam creating a 'knife edge'. The top edge is usually topstitched at this point about ⅛" in from this upper seam and then the pocket is basted to the bag. The raw edges at the bottom and sides will be caught into the side and base seams.

If the pocket is to 'float' outside of the seam lines, then the side and bottom seam allowances will need to be turned in by ¼" and pressed, then the sides and bottom edges can be sewn onto the corresponding back section.

Sew first very close to the folded edge and then again ¼" in from this line of stitching, thus enclosing the raw edges inside the pocket – a neat and very easy finish! This pocket would be unlined, but if you prefer to line your floating pocket, then cut out two pieces of fabric, one outer and one lining, and sew them right sides together all around, leaving a turning gap in the bottom seam. Turn through to the right side, neaten the open gap and press flat. Topstitch the top edge only. Place the pocket onto the bag and topstitch the sides and base, closing the gap and attaching the pocket in one easy step.

You can add slip pockets to many of the bags in this book if you have need for them! I also like to make slip pockets with a 'faux' binding: the outer pocket piece is cut to one size but the lining is a little longer, generally ½" extra.

The top edges are stitched together and the seam allowance is pressed up towards the lining, then the lining is flipped back over the seam allowance and back down the other side. The bottom edges should meet perfectly and you will be left with around ¼" of the lining showing on the right side, creating a gorgeous 'faux binding'. A line of topstitching just into this binding completes the illusion that a separate binding has been applied, and it's a lovely opportunity to add a little colour accent to an otherwise quite plain bag. Slip pockets with faux binding can be substituted for any regular slip pocket, so have fun and make each bag uniquely yours!

# PATCHWORK TECHNIQUES FOR 'MAKING FABRIC'

I've been a patchworker for pretty much as long as I can remember. Aged 6 or 7 my teacher, Miss Jenkins, rewarded my hard work in class with a pile of pretty scrap fabrics and paper hexagons, and taught me how to make 'English style' patchwork or 'English paper piecing'. I've been hooked ever since! Since those early steps I have tried almost every style of patchwork and quilting and, I've got to be honest here, I still haven't met a technique I didn't love.

All patchwork techniques share one common aim, to create larger pieces of fabric from smaller ones, often scraps. The aim is universal: turn tiny offcuts/scraps/'waste' into a serviceable and usable piece of fabric which can then be turned into bedding, clothing, accessories and bags! Everywhere there is fabric there are techniques to patchwork leftovers and give new life to worn or faded cloth. Every culture has its methods, and every generation has sought to stretch precious commodities like yarn, thread and fabric to its maximum lifespan. I have drawn on some of these methods to create new fabric and to give life to your handmade bags!

I have made every bag with fabric "plain and simple". Just raid your stash for ½ metres, fat quarters (18" x 21" cuts) or fat eighths (9" x 21" cuts) and make the bags with "whole" fabric.

You can also take a patchwork route and make your own fabric from scraps! I've used four different traditional patchwork techniques to "make" fabric:

## ENGLISH PAPER PIECING

The quintessential English method of hand sewing patchwork involves tacking or basting fabric to paper shapes, often small hexagons but also diamonds and other geometric shapes, before they are whip-stitched together.

1. Photocopy or trace about ⅓ the number of shapes you require for your project. Do this onto sturdy paper (manila envelopes were always a favourite) or very thin card.

2. Cut fabric approximately ¼" bigger on all sides and then pin a paper shape to the wrong side of the fabric, ensuring the seam allowance is even on all sides. Use a fabric-safe glue stick to glue the seam allowance to the paper template, folding the edge of the fabric against the paper and creating crisp, accurate corners. Create a whole bunch of these patches, until your supply of paper shapes is exhausted, and then start sewing the shapes together.

3. Place two shapes right sides together and align the edges you wish to join. Use a single piece of sewing thread and a sharp sewing needle. Knot the thread to start and make tiny stitches to join the patches 'whipping' the edges together. Make sure your stitches only pick up a few threads of fabric from each patch. At the end of the seam work a couple of stitches on top of each other and fasten off your thread or add another patch and continue stitching.

4 Continue adding patches until your 'fabric' is big enough (plus a little extra on all sides) to fit your templates.

5 Remove all papers: if the glue is very dry and difficult to remove try running a pin under the seam allowance to loosen it or spritz with a tiny amount of water to soften the glue.

6 Remove the paper shapes. You can reuse them to create a larger piece of 'fabric' or to use in another project.

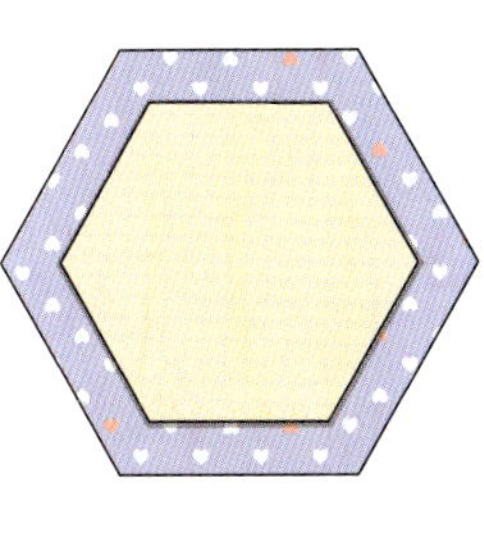

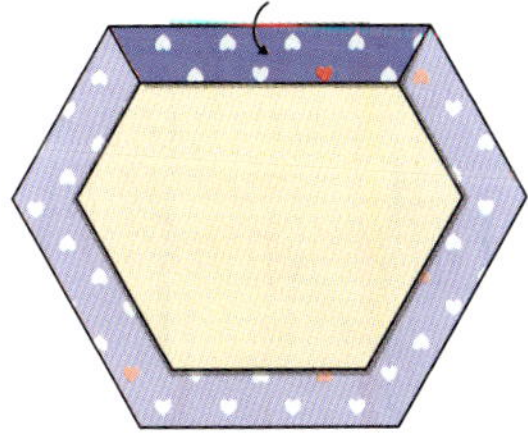

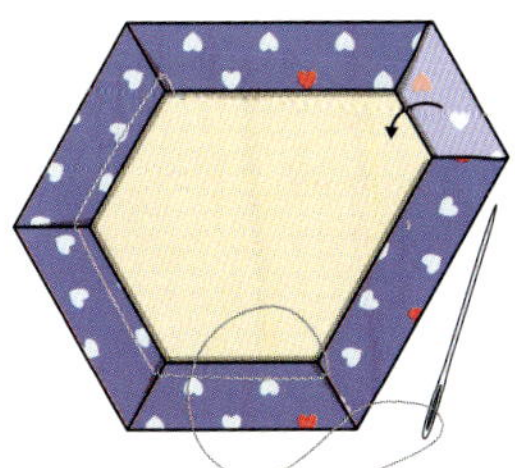

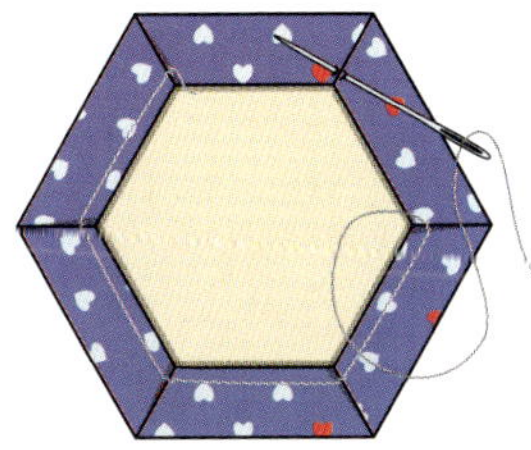

7 Either cut your fabric shapes out and then fuse to wadding or interfacing and then quilt, or interface/layer the patchwork, quilt it and then cut your templates from the quilted patchwork.

## A MODERN, QUICKER METHOD OF EPP

1 ↓ Spritz your fabrics with spray starch and iron dry.

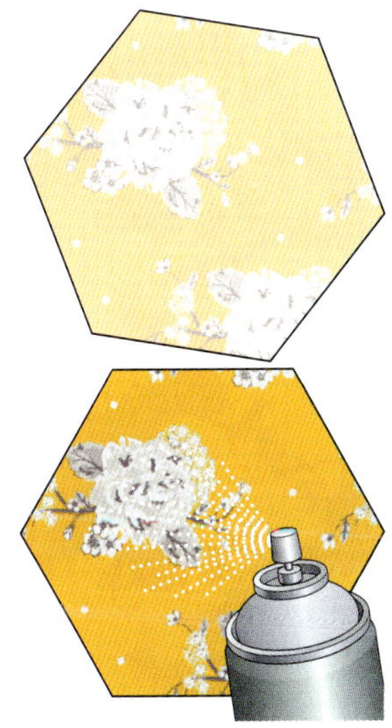

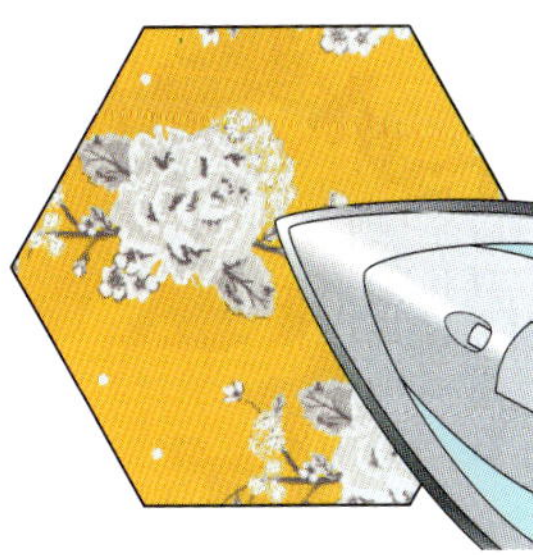

2 Cut out your patches as before but instead of gluing them to the templates use a needle and thread to catch the corners of the fabric only.

*Continues overleaf*

3 ↓ Iron the shape well to set the basting, leave to cool, then remove the basting.

4 Arrange your hexagons onto a piece of lightweight, fusible interfacing or batting, right sides facing up, and fuse in place. Make sure the edges are butted but not overlapping.

5 ↓ Use a zigzag or decorative stitch on your sewing machine to sew the hexagons together, making sure that the stitching holds down the patches effectively.

I've included templates for hexagons with a ½" side, a 1" side and a 2" side (on the pullout templates sheet), these sizes should work for a variety of fabrics and to match with the scale of the project you are working on. If time is short and your scraps are bigger, use the larger templates!

## STRING PIECING

String piecing is a very old technique used in a lot of old American quilts. This technique involves sewing lots of very thin strips of fabric to a foundation, usually calico but can also be paper (which is later removed) wadding or interfacing. Strips are often added at a 30- or 45-degree angle to the edge to create some lovely movement in the patchwork.

1 Start with a square or rectangular foundation a little bigger than you need and draw a line from corner to corner or at whatever angle you want the strips sewn in.

2 ↓ Lay one strip of fabric against the line, right side up, and add a second, right sides together, and then sew through the fabric and foundation; flip open and press and continue adding strips until the foundation is covered.

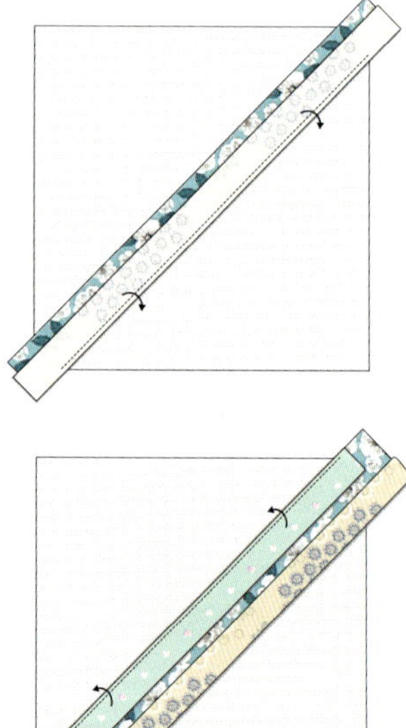

3 When the patchwork is complete, press and then trim the piece back to the required size or shape. If your fabric strips aren't long enough simply join strips of the same print (or a different print ... be daring!) and continue.

**The More You Know!**

A lot of modern sewers are using their selvedges (the narrow strip at the side of your fabric which displays the colour dots/manufacturers information) for string quilted projects. Fabric manufacturers have gotten in on the act and now many of them produce particularly decorative selvedges which really are too good to waste! Use all selvedges or take a mix-and-match approach. Quilters from yesteryear would approve, I have no doubt!

## BORO

Boro is a patchwork and mending tradition that comes from Japan. It developed out of a necessity to make woven hemp clothes last longer by patching the inevitable holes and worn areas with patches of indigo dyed cloth reinforced with sashiko or running stitches. This ancient technique grew out of a scarcity of cotton cloth and a reliance on less durable hemp cloth. Worn areas on clothing were covered with a raw-edged patch of cloth and then running stitches were added to reinforce the mending. Over the years more and more patches were added until the garment was almost covered. Since then, it has become an art form and a well-loved style of patchwork. Many makers use traditional or reproduction indigo prints, shibori dyed cloth or Japanese-style fabrics but this technique can be used with regular quilting fabrics and solids too.

1 ↓ You will need a foundation to stitch onto. I use quilters calico or butter muslin if I want a lighter cloth, or you can use wadding/batting or fusible foam for a heavier-weight result. Fusible foundations work particularly well, as you build up your panel without stitching to begin with and the fusible foundation keeps everything in place.

2 Cut or tear roughly rectangular or square patches of assorted sizes from your chosen fabrics.

3 ↓ Arrange them in an overlapping but irregular arrangement. Choose different scales of print for interest and also vary the size of the patches. Fuse the fabrics to the foundation or use large tacking stitches or even a fabric-safe glue stick to hold the patches where you have placed them.

4 Once you've created a pleasing arrangement (it doesn't have to be complete at this stage), you can start the fun stitching to attach the patches to the foundation. Use thicker than sewing thread. (I like to use traditional sashiko thread in white, ecru or navy, or you can use two or three strands of embroidery floss in a suitable needle.) Variegated threads look particularly effective. You can go as simple as working a running stitch about ⅛" in from the raw edges on all the patches, as this is enough to hold the patches in place, but add more stitching if you can!

5 ↓ Work vertical or horizontal lines of stitches, spirals or diagonal crosshatching. You could even use an element in the fabric, such as a small polka dot, and work your stitches around this motif.

6 Boro is a technique where the more stitching you add, the richer and more complex looking the piece will be. Once you've worked the base layer, you can add a few 'floating' patches, which go over the top of already-stitched areas. Add more running stitch detail over these floating patches.

7 Once your boro panel is completed you will need to trace a line around the template shape.

8 Next, use a narrow zigzag stitch on your machine to sew very closely just inside this line. This zigzag stitching is necessary to capture any hand sewing, as in a few moments you will cut the shape out and we need to prevent threads coming loose. Anywhere you plan to stitch (such as box bottoms/corners) you will need to zigzag.

## IMPROV OR CRUMB QUILTING/LIBERATED PIECING/CRAZY PATCHWORK

There are so many different permutations of this kind of patchwork, but they all have something of a 'no rules' approach which can feel at the same time rather freeing and also a little terrifying! All these styles have a sort of 'crazy paving' approach and all of the methods involved sewing odd-shaped pieces of fabric together, either by hand or machine and often to a foundation of paper or a light calico. Edges can be trimmed to make adding additional pieces of fabric easier, but if all else fails a piece can be 'appliquéd' to cover an awkward hole!

**FOR CRUMB QUILTING:**

1 ↓ Cut fabric into rough rectangle/square/strip pieces.

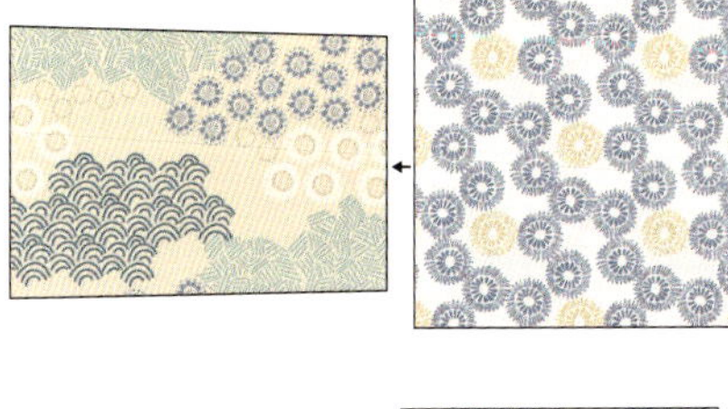

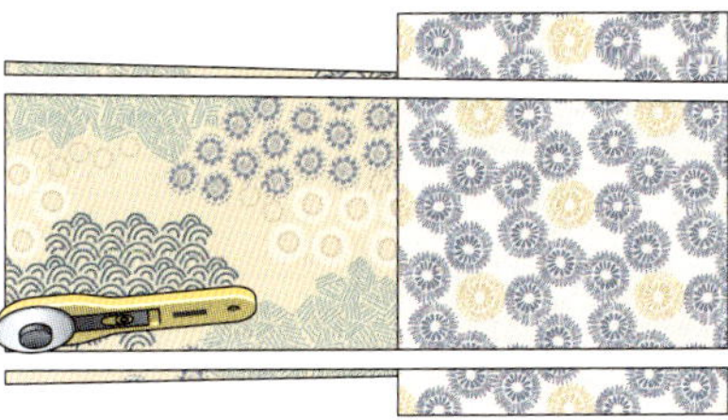

2 ↓ Sew two pieces that will fit together, then add a third, either to the opposite side or the top or bottom.

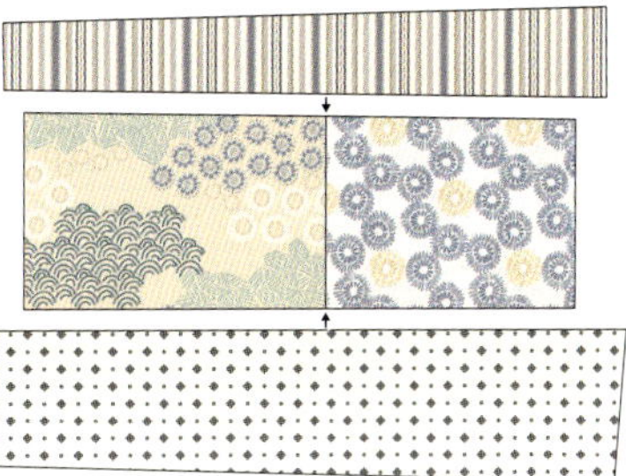

3 Add more pieces or, my preference, make a bunch of these patches, ideally some roughly square and some roughly rectangular, and then join them.

4 ↓ At times you will need to straighten an edge up or trim a patch down to make it fit. You're going for random, not regular. Be brave – you can do it!

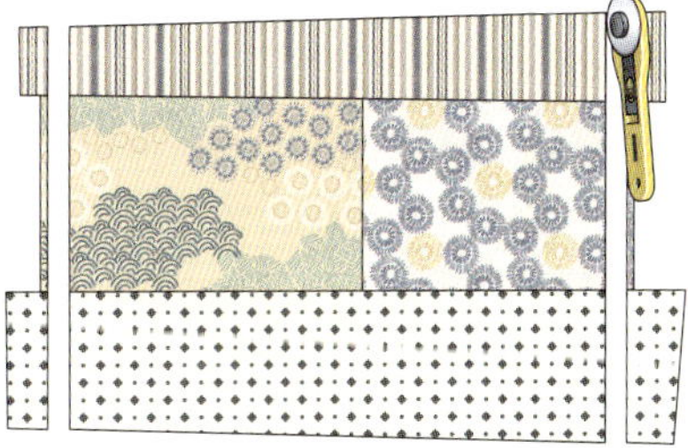

*Continues overleaf*

**LIBERATED PIECING** or **IMPROV QUILTING** are different names for much the same thing: quilting/patchwork without the rules or a set pattern in mind. There are a number of ways to achieve this.

1 Create familiar patchwork units and blocks but with a free hand and a very liberal attitude towards points and accuracy.

2 Piece the units together and trim if needed to fit them together OR start with a centre shape like a square or rectangle and add pieces to the sides, log-cabin style.

3 Add in some pre-pieced sections for greater interest. Make some traditional patchwork, like a nine patch block or squares, but then cut through the block at a casual angle and re-piece the block, adding in extra strips.

**CRAZY PATCHWORK** is usually worked on a fabric foundation. I like to use calico but you can also sew directly to wadding, batting or light interfacing.

1 I like to start somewhere near the centre with a five-sided roughly cut shape.

2 Place that onto the foundation, right side up, and place a second shape, strip or square rights sides touching.

3 Sew a ¼″ seam and flip them open. I'll keep adding shapes in this way, working out from the centre.

4 If you box yourself into a corner and a shape is very awkward to add, you could always appliqué a patch over the top; just finger press a seam allowance along the covering edge and sew it in place. If the patch you need to add seems rather large, you can always sew a couple of pieces of fabric together and then add them on.

5 Join several crazy patch 'blocks' together to make fabric large enough for your project.

# PROJECTS

# 'DON'T SHOOT THE MESSENGER' BAG

I make more messenger bags than any other type of bag. They are sleek, stylish, useful, and the boxy shape can be made to look rather masculine, so is perfect when I'm making a bag for myself (but also for my girlfriends!). The front flap and back slip pocket are perfect places to show off a big print – and don't worry if you end up having to cut off part of the design as it will still look amazing!

I've picked one main large-scale outer fabric for lots of impact – a print from Japan featuring cranes and dragons. A floral pattern would also look beautiful, but so too would a plain navy wool or faux leather. I've contrasted the main print with a toning solid to give the large-scale print room to breathe and frame it nicely – choose something that will help the main fabric to pop but also allow the eye to rest. I've used a third fabric for the lining.

**Gather your supplies! You will need...**

- Main outer fabric A (at least 0.5m, or double that if using a very large spaced-out motif that you wish to fussy cut)
  Front flap: 10″ x 9½″ (landscape), fussy cutting any special motifs
  Inner flap: 9½″ x 5½″ (landscape)
  Bellows pocket: 14½″ x 8½″, again centring any special motifs
  Back slip pocket: 10½″ x 9½″ (landscape)
  Two bag sides: each 3½″ x 11½″ (portrait)
  Base: 3½″ x 10½″
  Two D ring attachments: each 2″ x 3″. If you're making your own shoulder strap, cut/join 2″ x 60″

- Contrast fabric B (0.5m)
  Front and back panels: each 11½″ x 10½″ (portrait)
  One strip: 2″ x 12″ to bind the slip pocket
  One strip: 1½″ x 28″ to cover the piping cord, if using

- Lining fabric C (0.5m)
  Outer flap lining: 10″ x 9½″
  Inner flap lining: 9½″ x 5½″
  Bellows pocket lining: 14½″ x 8½″
  Back slip pocket: 9½″ x 10½″
  Inner bag lining (front and back): 10½″ x 11½″
  Two side panels: each 3½″ x 11½″
  One base panel: 3½″ x 10½″
  Two 9″ squares for the internal zipped pocket
  Two rectangles each 2″ x 3″ for the D ring attachment linings. If you're making your own shoulder strap, cut/piece 2″ x 60″

*Continues overleaf*

I used a ready-made leather shoulder strap that I bought online, but you could follow general instructions on page 32 to make an adjustable shoulder strap in matching fabrics, if you prefer. You won't need extra fabrics to do this as you'll have enough left over.

## FINISHED SIZE

10" x 11" x 3"

## SKILL LEVEL

Intermediate

## SKILLS USED

This is a really fun-to-sew bag for any maker with a bit of bag-making experience. It's not a difficult bag to make by any means, but there are a number of processes and a few fancy add-ons which take it into intermediate level. You might do some fussy cutting (see page 25), depending on your choice of fabric; you'll use fusible foam and interfacing; make a letterbox zip and a slip pocket. You'll also make a 'bellows' pocket and a piped edge to your flap (although this step is optional); you'll also do some quilting and topstitching. As I said, lots of processes, but oh my goodness, so worth it!

- Medium-weight fusible interfacing (0.5m)
  Interface all lining pieces, cutting the interfacing ½" smaller than fabric dimensions.
- Bosal In-R-Form or other thin fusible foam (0.5m)
  Cut fusible foam for the outer main flap, front and back panels, sides and base, cutting the foam ½" smaller than the fabric dimensions. Fuse the foam to the wrong side of the appropriate pieces.
- Threads to quilt, construct and topstitch
- Fabric-safe pen or pencil
- 1m narrow piping cord (optional)
- Two 1½" aperture D rings in your choice of metal or plastic finish
- One leather/faux leather or fabric removable shoulder strap (or to make your own: one 1½" aperture strap slider and two 1½" aperture swivel clasps)
- One magnetic snap or a sew-on snap closure for the main bag
- One 8" zip to match the lining fabric
- Small rounded object (a small dish or saucer to round the lower corners of the bag flaps)

## LET'S MAKE THE BAG!

1 ↓ You should already have the outer sections (front, back, sides, base and main flap fused to foam). Mark the quilting lines with a fabric-safe pen and quilt as desired (I played around with single and double crosshatch quilting). Trim any loose threads, then remove the mark lines once the quilting is complete.

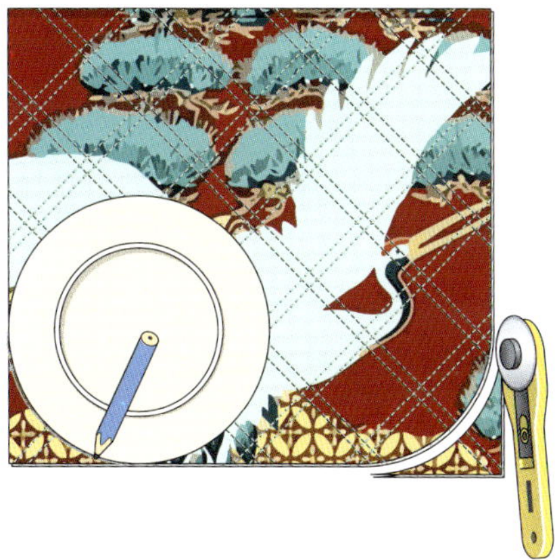

2 ↓ Take the quilted front flap and the interfaced front flap lining. Use a round object to round the bottom two corners, then trim away the excess fabric. Find the centre bottom on the lining and measure up 1½" from this point. Apply the male half of the magnetic snap, keeping the female half safe.

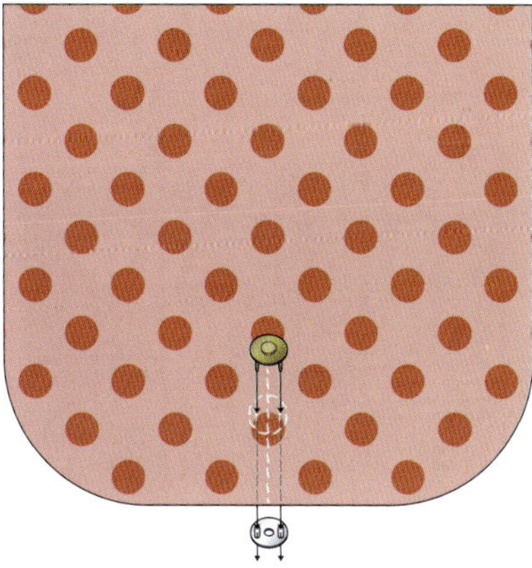

3 If adding piping to the flap edge, install the zipper foot on your sewing machine. Wrap the 1½" x 28" fabric strip around the piping cord and bring the raw edges together flat. Sew close to the piping cord, but not too close yet! Trim the fabric back from the raw edges to within ¼" of the stitching line. Pin the covered cord around the sides and lower edge of the quilted front flap, raw edges matching. Snip into the fabric at the curved corners to help the fabric 'bend' (don't snip through the stitches, just up to them).

4 ↓ Now sew the piping cord to the front flap, sewing on or near the original line of stitching. Trim the cord ends. Layer the quilted flap with the lining, right sides together, and carefully pin.

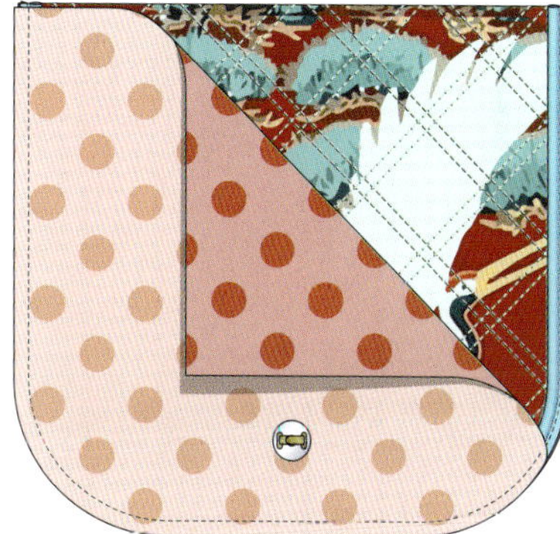

5 ↓ Now sew the sides and bottom seams as close to the piping cord as you can, a little closer than your previous efforts. Turn the flap through to the right side and press. Baste the top raw edges together to hold in place. Set aside the completed flap.

*Continues overleaf*

6 Make the inner flap. The outer fabric is just fabric, the lining is interfaced. Smooth out the corners with your round object, then align both pieces, right sides together, and sew around the top, sides and base, leaving a small gap open in the top seam. Turn through to the right side and press. While pressing, bring the open gap together neatly and press but don't stitch it yet! Set the flap aside.

7 Make the bellows pocket. The outer pocket piece is just fabric, the lining is interfaced. Place the female part of the magnetic snap on the outer bellows pocket piece, 4¼" up from the bottom raw edge and right in the centre (place a little interfacing behind the magnetic snap if the fabric is flimsy). Place the outer and lining fabrics right sides together and sew all around, leaving a small gap for turning in one of the side edges. Turn to the right side and press, then topstitch along the top edge only.

8 ↓ On the quilted front panel, mark a line across the bottom 1" up from the raw edge using a fabric-safe pen. Also mark vertical lines 1" in from the sides. Pin the pocket piece to the sides first, aligning the sides of the pocket with the vertical lines, then topstitch in place.

9 ↓ Next, make deep and even pleats in both sides to make the pocket lie flat against the bag front. Pin the bottom edge, then topstitch it in place. Position the pocket flap over the bellows pocket, centring it (it should be 1" down from the top edge). Make sure the flap won't interfere with the workings of the magnetic snap, which should sit at least ½" below it. Topstitch the flap in place. You could add a KAM snap or a sew-on popper to the pocket/flap if you wish, but I didn't. Set the back front aside.

10 ↓ Make the back of the bag. Place the back slip pocket and lining wrong sides together and baste around the outer edges ⅛" in from the raw edges. Use the 2" strip of contrast fabric folded in half to bind the top edge of the pocket, 'quilt style'. Once completed, baste the slip pocket to the quilted back panel of the bag.

**11** Make the D ring attachments. Take the two 2" x 3" interfaced lining pieces and the corresponding outer pieces and place them in pairs, right sides facing. Sew the long edges, turn through, press and topstitch the side edges. Thread each one through a D ring and baste the raw edges together. Set aside.

**12** ↓ Make the outer bag. Lay the bag front and back, quilted base and sides in a 'cross' shape as shown. Sew the bag front to the base and then the back to the base, starting and finishing seam allowances ¼" in from the corners. Use a ¼" seam allowance throughout. Sew the sides in next, sewing from the very top down to a ¼" off the corner.

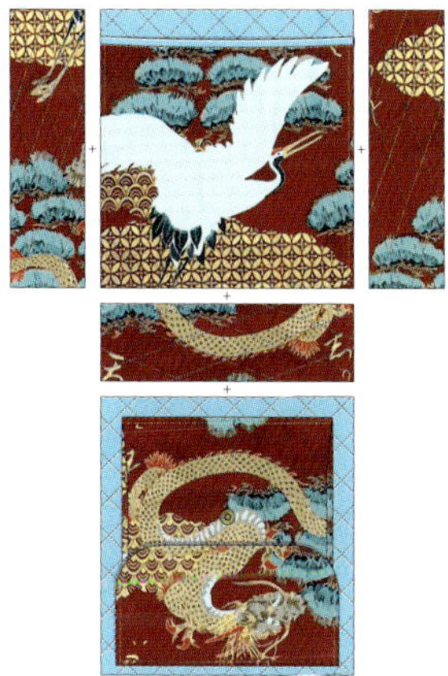

**13** ↓ Finally, sew across the short base seams from corner to corner. Turn the bag through to the right side and press. Centre the D ring attachments to the bag sides and baste in place. Place the bag flap, right sides touching, to the bag back and baste in place. Set aside.

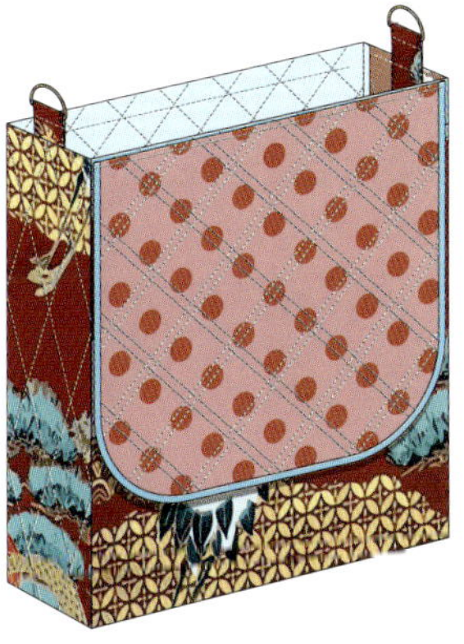

**14** Make the bag lining. Make the internal letterbox zip pocket first. Follow general instructions (see page 30). Place the letterbox outline 1½" down from the top edge and 1" in from the sides of one 9" pocket square. Position the pocket piece on the lining back piece, right sides facing and top raw edges aligned, making sure the pocket piece is central. Sew around the letterbox outline, then snip through and 'post your pocket', press then pin and sew the zip into place.

**15** Finally, sew the remaining 9" square pocket piece to the back of the pocket only, then baste the top edges of the pocket and the back lining piece together.

**16** Make up the lining in exactly the same way as the bag outer, but leave a 4" gap in one of the base seams. Leave the lining wrong side out.

**17** Place the outer bag inside the lining, making sure that the bag flap is on the same side as the zippered internal pocket (these are both on the back of the bag). Align the top edges of the bag and pin or hold them together with quilters clips. Sew around the top of the bag using a generous ¼" seam allowance. Turn the right side through the gap in the lining, press and then close the gap in the lining by hand or machine.

**18** Press the top edge of the bag neatly, then topstitch very close to the top edge to finish the bag!

**19** Clip the ready-made shoulder strap to the bag, or if you're making your own, follow the general instructions on page 32, using the 2" x 60" lengths of outer and lining fabric. Or why not use 1½" webbing for a quick-and-easy sew-your-own option!

# 'DON'T SHOOT THE MESSENGER' BAG

**Now let's make the project using the patchwork techniques on pages 38–45.**

**BORO**

Focus your boro piecing on the front flap, where it has maximum impact.

**IMPROV**

Create 'wonky' flying geese and edge with fabric strips.

**STRING PIECE**

String piece at a 45° angle to create movement on the flap.

OPPOSITE: **HEXI**

# ESSENTIAL DAY BAG

My essential day bag is a stylish and sophisticated make with elegantly curved edges. The bag is nice and roomy for daytime essentials, and there's also a simple slip pocket inside for extra storage. You could add a letterbox zip to the back of the bag if you wanted, but I chose to keep the lines simple and elegant. The contrast gusset and flap binding are a lovely opportunity to show off your style and make a bag that's as unique as you are. The tongue lock is a quick way to close the bag, but you could easily substitute a magnetic snap or even a button and loop. I used a ready-made leather shoulder strap, but you could very easily substitute a webbing or fabric strap using another pattern in the book.

## FINISHED SIZE

13″ x 10″ x 3½″

## SKILL LEVEL

Intermediate

## SKILLS USED

There are a few more processes to make this bag, hence the intermediate tag, but don't be put off if you're more of a beginner. Take it steady and use the techniques section of this book (pages 24–45) to learn what you need. You'll use a paper pattern to cut out your fabrics, you'll also use fusible foam, do some quilting, make a lining with a slip pocket, create a binding edge, put in a gusset and sew on a tongue lock.

**Gather your supplies! You will need...**

- Main outer fabric A (0.5m)
  For the bag front, back and flap front
- Main outer fabric B (0.5m)
  For the flap binding, bag gusset and D ring attachments
- Lining fabric C (0.5m)
  For the flap, inside and internal slip pocket
- Thread to match your fabrics, and also thread to match the tongue lock
- Hand-sewing needle
- Bosal In-R-Form single-sided fusible foam
- Medium-weight fusible interfacing
- 505 basting spray (optional)
- Fabric-safe pen or pencil
- Two 1½″ aperture D rings in your chosen metal or plastic finish
- One sew-on tongue lock
- One ready-made detachable shoulder strap, about 60″ in length
- Pattern pieces for the front, back and flap copied onto sturdy paper (see the pullout template sheet)

## LET'S MAKE THE BAG!

1 From fusible foam cut a bag front, a bag back and a flap. All these pieces are cut to the finished size without additional seam allowance.

2 Fuse the foam pieces to the wrong side of fabric A, leaving 1" between all pieces. Cut the fabric out, adding a ¼" seam allowance to all pieces – I do this by eye, but you can mark it if you prefer.

3 Cut a piece of lining fabric for the flap that is 1" bigger on all sides. Use 505 basting spray to fuse this fabric to the back of the flap, creating a 'sandwich'. The pretty side of the flap should be showing, as well as the pretty side of the lining fabric on the back.

4 From fusible foam cut a 3" x 34" strip. From fabric B cut a 3½" x 34" strip. Fuse the foam to the wrong side of the fabric B strip, centring the foam and leaving ¼" of fabric free on both long edges.

5 ↓ Mark your desired quilting lines on the outer bag, flap and gusset. I quilted a 1" diamond crosshatch on the front and back pieces, horizontal lines on the gusset and vertical lines on the flap. For the gusset and flap I only marked the first few lines ½" apart as a guide to get me started. I used the width of the sewing machine foot thereafter.

6 Quilt the bag front and back panels, the gusset and the flap. The flap is the only part of the bag that has a lining attached before quilting!

7 Finish the flap, only trimming the excess fabric from the sides and curved lower edge right up to the inner foam. Trim the fabric at the back to within ¼" of the foam.

8 ↓ From fabric B cut one strip 2½" x WOF (width of fabric) and fold in half lengthways, wrong sides together, then press, making a binding strip. Use this fabric strip to bind the sides and curved lower edge of the flap.

9 Working on the right side of the flap, align the raw edges of the binding with the raw edge of the flap, pin the binding in place carefully, easing it around the curved corners, and sew with a ¼" seam allowance. Notch the seam allowance around the curved corners with sharp scissors to help the fabric 'bend', then turn the binding to the lining side of the flap. Pin it in place, then either hand sew the binding to the lining side or, working from the front, machine sew 'in the ditch' to attach the binding. Set the flap aside.

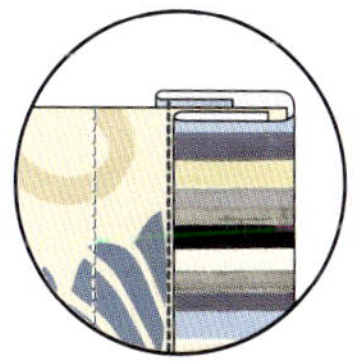

*Continues overleaf*

**10** ↓ Make the main body of the bag. Take the front and back bag panels and mark the centre position at the bottom of the pieces. Find the centre of the gusset on both sides and mark. Pin the gusset around the bag front, starting at the centre bottom of the bag and then centre of the gusset, pinning fabric to fabric and avoiding going through the foam. You will need lots of pins, particularly at the curved corners. Work up to the top edge – there is excess gusset and it will hang over, but who doesn't love wiggle room? Now starting again at the centre bottom, pin the remaining side of the gusset to the bag front. Sew the gusset to the bag front using a ¼" seam allowance.

**11** ↓ Carefully trim the excess gusset from the end so that it is perfectly level with the top of the bag front.

**12** Repeat the process as above with the back of the bag, matching the centre bottom and the tops first and then pinning in between for the perfect fit. Sew the back to the gusset. Turn the bag to the right side, then carefully press the seams.

**13** Pin the flap to the back of the bag, right sides together and using an ⅛" seam allowance.

**14** → Make and attach the D rings. From fabric B cut one 3½" x 7" strip. Interface the whole piece on the wrong side with fusible interfacing. Fold the rectangle in half, right sides together, and sew the long edge using a ¼" seam allowance, then turn through and press. The strips should be 1½" x 7" at this stage. Topstitch both long raw edges, then cut two 3" lengths from this piece. Fold the attaching loops through the D rings and baste the raw edges together. I also like to sew very close to the straight edge of the D ring using a zipper foot to get as close as possible. This extra row of stitching helps the D ring to stay in position when using the bag. I find it so annoying when D rings twist and turn!

**15** Baste the D rings to the outer bag, centring the attachments to the gusset.

**16** ↓ Hand sew the tongue lock to the bag. Position the upper part of the lock on the flap, centre it and hand sew in place using matching thread and a backstitch. Attach the lower part of the lock to the upper part, letting the lower part sit where it naturally falls with the bag sitting on the table. Make sure it's central and not distorting the bag. Place a mark where the lock sits, then remove the lower part of the lock and sew it to the front of the bag using a backstitch.

**17** Make the lining. From lining fabric (C) cut a bag front and back using the pattern pieces and add a ¼" seam allowance by eye. Also cut a 3½" x 34" strip of fabric C for the gusset lining and also two rectangles 9½" x 7" (landscape) for the slip pocket. Interface the main front and back lining pieces and the gusset using medium-weight fusible interfacing and set aside.

**18** Make the slip pocket. Place the two pocket pieces right sides together and pin. Sew around the perimeter, leaving a 3" gap in one side. Use a ¼" seam allowance. Turn the pocket through to the right side, then turn the seam allowances on the gap inwards to neaten. Press the pocket and topstitch the upper edge.

**19** Position the pocket onto the lining back piece 2" down from the top edge and central. Pin in place, then topstitch the pocket. I like to do a little triangle of reinforcing stitches at the top of the pocket.

**20** Make the lining up as you did the bag outer. Pin the gusset to the lining front carefully in place and sew first. Trim the tops of the gusset evenly, then pin and sew the gusset to the back of the bag, leaving a 4" turning gap in the bottom seam.

**21** Place the outer bag inside the lining so that the right sides are touching. Match the upper raw edges and pin, then sew around the top of the bag using a ⅜" seam allowance. Turn the bag to the right side through the turning gap in the lining. Close the gap by hand or machine.

**22** Align and press the top edge of the bag, then topstitch around the top of the bag ¼" down from the top edge.

**23** Clip your ready-made (or handmade) shoulder strap to the bag and try it on for size. Fabulous!

# ESSENTIAL DAY BAG

**Now let's make the project using the patchwork techniques on pages 38–45.**

**BORO**

If time is short, create a small piece of boro for the flap only.

**STRING PIECE**

String piece the gusset and flap and contrast with a plain front and back.

**HEXI**

Use mid-sized hexis on the bag front and back only – create a pop with contrasting flap and gusset.

**OPPOSITE: IMPROV**

# JAPANESE RICE BAG (KOMEBUKURO)

These Japanese rice bags are so cute and easy to make. I use them for a multitude of things: gift bags, storage in my workroom, even lunch bags! The cube shape lends itself very well to showcasing some lovely piecing, boro, machine embroidery or patchwork. You could also fussy cut special fabrics and use a different print for each side. The size of the squares can vary, but don't go too small or they get a bit fiddly. I've included how to make the little tulip-shaped cord ends – they are fun to make and you can add them to any bag with cords for a decorative touch!

## FINISHED SIZE

7½" x 7½" x 7½"

## SKILL LEVEL

Beginner

## SKILLS USED

You'll do some quilting, make a simple box-shaped bag, make tabs and insert a lining. You'll also learn to make decorative cord ends!

**Gather your supplies! You will need...**

- Fabric A (0.25m)

**For the outer bag and tabs**

- Fabric B (0.5m)

**For the lining and tabs**

- Two assorted matching scraps (four 3½" squares for the cord ends)
- Quilt batting/wadding
- Medium-weight fusible interfacing
- 2m decorative cord
- Hand-sewing needle and thread
- Thread to match your fabrics
- Fabric-safe pen or pencil

## LET'S MAKE THE BAG!

1 From fabrics A and B, wadding and interfacing, cut five 8″ squares each (a total of 20 squares).

2 Layer the outer fabric A squares with the wadding squares: pin the wadding and fabric together, pretty side of the fabric uppermost, then mark some simple quilting lines. Quilt as desired – I quilted diagonal lines on the four sides and a double crosshatch on the base square. Remove the mark lines once the quilting is completed.

3 From fabrics A and B cut four tabs each 2″ x 3″ (a total of 8 rectangles). Pair an A and a B tab, right sides together, and sew both long edges using a ¼″ seam allowance. Turn to the right side, press and topstitch down the long sides. Make four in total.

4 ↓ Position the five quilted outer squares in a cross, making sure any directional fabric or quilting is placed appropriately. Sew the four sides to the base square first, starting and finishing the seam ¼″ in from the raw edges and backstitching to secure.

5 → ↑ Bring the sides up to match and start sewing from the top of each corner. Sew down to the ¼″ mark and backstitch. Turn the bag through to the right side and press.

6 ↓ Now find the centres of all four sides and mark each with a pin. Fold the tabs in half, lining to lining, and baste the tabs to the mid-points on all four sides.

7 ↓ Interface the five lining squares. Sew them into a cube shape just as you did the outer bag, but remember to leave a 3″ gap in one seam for turning.

*Continues overleaf*

8 ↓ Put the outer bag into the lining so that the right sides are touching. Pin the top edge together, matching the corners carefully. Sew around the top of the bag using a ¼" seam allowance. Turn the bag through to the right side and press the top edge carefully. Sew the gap in the lining closed, by hand or machine.

9 Topstitch around the top of the bag.

10 Cut the cord into two lengths of 1m.

11 ↓ Thread the cords through the tabs, starting and finishing in opposite corners. Knot the ends of the cord together.

12 ↓ Make decorative cord covers. Take one 3½" square and fold it in half, right sides together. Sew down the side opposite the fold using a ¼" seam allowance. Carefully turn the tube halfway through so that the right side is outside and the raw ends match up.

13 Use a needle and thread to hand sew a running stitch ½″ down from the raw ends.

14 ↓ Place the tube over the knotted cord, folded edge uppermost, and draw up the running stitches close to the knotted cord. Pull the folded edge back down over the knot (at this stage it looks like a little bell).

15 → Using the same needle and thread, bring the opposite sides of the little bell together in the centre and hand stitch a couple of times. Now bring the remaining two opposite sides together in the middle and make a couple of stitches. Bury the thread in the centre of the flower and clip the threads. Make a second cord cover for the other knotted end.

Odif

# JAPANESE RICE BAG (KOMEBUKURO)

**Now let's make the project using the patchwork techniques on pages 38–45.**

**HEXI**
Make hexi 'rosettes' and appliqué them to the side panels.

**IMPROV**
Create 'wonky' log-cabin blocks for each side of the bag.

**STRING PIECE**
String piece each side of the bag separately.

**OPPOSITE: BORO**

# 'KEEPING IT CRAFTY' CADDY

Welcome to your new crafting best friend! Seriously, you're going to love this very useful storage caddy with 10 pockets and a huge internal space to cram with all sorts of crafting goodies. This project is a great place to practise your pockets too – there are three different types: lined and bound slip pockets; unlined bound vinyl pockets; and concertina or bellows pockets. Feel free to change up the pockets if you wish and use these methods to add or adapt the other bags in this book. I've also included a fun hack using cotton webbing for the handles – it came out of necessity as I only had cream in stock and it was a bit too creamy to work with my fabrics, so I added a wide folded strip of coordinating fabric to the centre and topstitched it in place. The handles went from unmatched to snatched in about 5 minutes flat!

## FINISHED SIZE

12" x 8" x 6"

## SKILL LEVEL

Confident beginner level with some intermediate skills. This is one to practise on!

## SKILLS USED

You'll do some quilting, make different kinds of pockets, sew a quilt-style binding, use vinyl, make handles using webbing and insert a lining.

**Gather your supplies! You will need...**

- Main outer fabric A (0.5m)

**For the main caddy and handles**

Base: 6½" x 12½"
Front and back: two 8½" x 12½"
Ends: two 6½" x 8½"
Handles: three 2½" x 16" strips

- Contrast fabric B (0.25m)

**For the outer pockets**

Long concertina/bellows pocket: 6½" x 16½"
End slip pockets: two 6½" x 6½"

- Contrast fabric C (0.5m)

**For the lining**

Base: 6½" x 12½"
Front/back: two 8½" x 12½"
Ends: two 6½" x 8½"
Pocket linings: 6½" x 16½" (to line the bellows pocket), two 6½" x 6½" (to line the end slip pockets), two 6½" x 12½" (to line the internal slip pockets)

- Contrast fabric D (0.25m)
  Internal slip pockets: two 6½" x 12½"

- Contrast fabric E (stripe) (0.25m)

**For the pocket bindings**

Binding strips: three 2½" x WOF (width of fabric) strips. Fold and press, wrong sides together.

*Continues overleaf*

Colle Temporaire
Tijdelijke Lijm
TISSUS
FABRIC

## LET'S MAKE THE BAG!

1 Fuse all outer caddy pieces to the corresponding pieces of fusible foam, centring the fabric and ensuring that there is a ¼" margin all around. Mark your chosen quilting designs onto the fabric using the fabric-safe pen and then quilt as desired. Set aside.

2 ↓ Make the handles. Take the three 2½" x 16" strips of main fabric A and fold/press them in half down the centre, wrong sides together – do this lightly! Open out the fold and turn the raw outer edges in towards the centre, then crease and press again: this creates an approximately 1¼" neatened strip of fabric. Position one, right sides up, centrally on a 16" length of cotton webbing and pin in place, then topstitch very close to the folded fabric edge on both long edges. Repeat with a second strip and the other 16" handle, then cut the last folded strip into two 7" lengths (discard the remaining 2") and use to trim the 7" lengths of webbing. Set the handles aside.

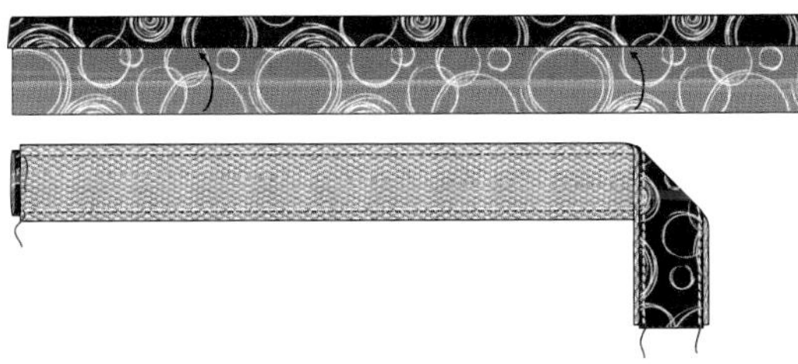

3 Make the internal slip pockets and the lining. Take one internal slip pocket cut from fabric D and one internal pocket lining and place wrong sides together, then pin or tack all edges together. Use a 2½" strip of binding fabric, and working from the lining side first, align the raw edges of the binding with the raw edges of the pocket top and sew with a ¼" seam allowance. Turn the folded binding towards the front/right side of the pocket and press with an iron. Topstitch the binding in place by sewing very close on the binding edge. Repeat for the second internal slip pocket.

*Continues overleaf*

- Clear vinyl (6½" x 12½")
- Medium-weight woven fusible interfacing (0.5m)
  Interface all fabric pockets, including the internal slip pockets (excluding the vinyl pocket) and interface all internal lining pieces for the main caddy
- Bosal In-R-Form fusible foam (0.5m)
  Base: 6" x 12"
  Front/back: two 8" x 12"
  Ends: two 6" x 8"
- 1½" wide cotton webbing (1.5m)
  Main handles: two 16" lengths
  End handles: two 7" lengths
- Thread to match your fabrics
- Fabric-safe pen or pencil
- Fabric-safe glue stick
- Sharpie pen
- Walking foot or non-stick foot for working with the vinyl

4 Baste the internal slip pockets to the corresponding lining pieces, then mark a line centrally down the middle of each pocket to divide it into two. Sew down this line, reinforcing the stitching at the top and bottom.

5 ↓ Lay the lining pieces out in a 'cross' as shown, then sew the edges together using a ⅜" seam allowance using the basic 'box bag' technique (see page 37). Leave an 8" turning gap in one of the base seams. I know this seems like a very large turning gap but you will need it. It's a lot of bag, a lot of pockets and the vinyl and interfacing make the whole thing quite stiff. Leave the lining wrong sides out and set aside.

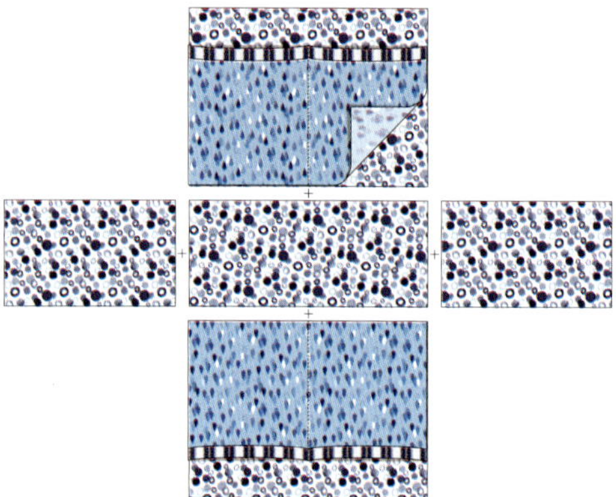

6 Make the external fabric slip pockets. Take one 6½" x 6½" outer slip pocket and one 6½" square of interfaced lining fabric and place wrong sides together, then baste around all 4 sides or pin. Use a 2½" strip of binding fabric to bind the top edge as before. Make two. Baste these pockets onto the quilted outer caddy ends. Set aside.

7 ↓ Make the vinyl pocket. Cut a strip of binding fabric 7" in length. Open up the binding and press the outer raw edges in to meet the centre crease (just as we did for the handle trims). This strip of fabric will be used to split the vinyl pocket in two. Use a Sharpie pen to mark the centre line up the middle of the vinyl. Apply glue stick to your folded fabric strip and cover the Sharpie pen line. Use quilters clips to hold it in place while the glue dries.

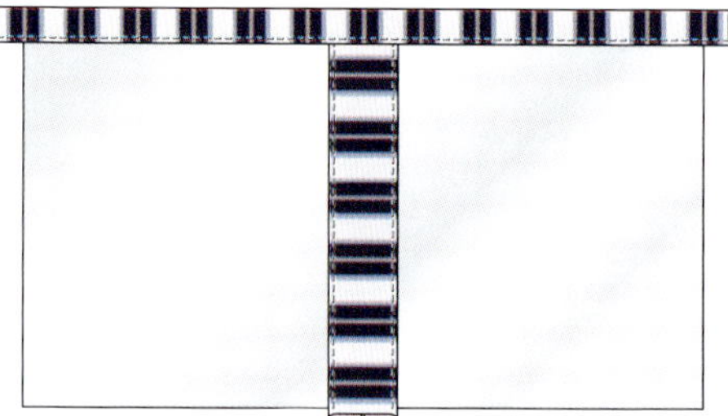

8 ↓ Use more of the binding fabric to bind the top edge of the vinyl pocket (I find using a walking foot or non-stick foot helps here), then sew down either side of the centre fabric strip to attach it properly. Baste the vinyl pocket to one of the front/back outer caddy pieces and set aside.

9 ↓ Make the concertina/bellows pocket. Prepare your bellows pocket exactly the same way as the lined/bound slip pockets, with the outer and lining basted together and then bound. Also mark the centre of the pocket with a line running top to bottom, using the fabric-safe pen.

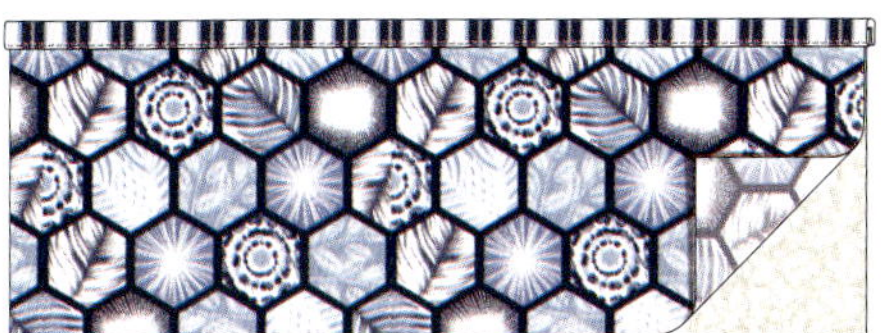

10 ↓ On the remaining quilted outer caddy front/back pieces, find and mark the centre line 1" in from both side edges. Mark the bottom of the quilted piece with pins at these points. Line up and baste the ends of the pocket with the ends of the main quilted piece (the pocket will be bulging dramatically forward at this point, but don't panic!).

11 Match the marked centre line on the pocket with the marked centre of the quilted front/back and pin in place. Sew from top to bottom on the marked line to anchor the pocket and divide it in two.

12 Now the folding begins! Fold around 1½" of pocket in towards the marked 1" line at each end of the pocket and pin in place. Also fold an equal amount in towards the centre line and pin in place. The bottom of the pocket should now be lying flat against the bottom of the main quilted piece. If it isn't, make a few small adjustments to get it flat. Baste the bottom edge of the pocket in place. Set aside.

13 Baste the handles onto the front, back and sides. The side handles are nestled against (but not overlapping) each other, and the main handles are central and approximately 3" apart.

14 ↓ Make the outer caddy up in the same way you made the lining. So use a ¼" seam allowance and the same basic box bag technique (see page 37). Do not leave a turning gap this time. Turn the bag through to the right side.

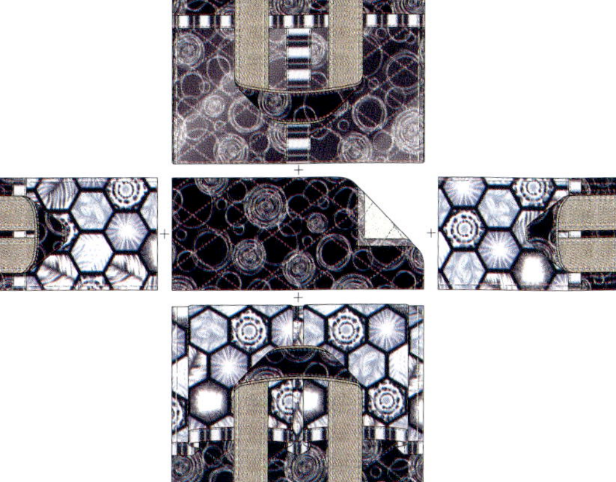

15 Place the outer bag into the lining, right sides together, and pin/clip around the top. Use a ⅜" seam allowance to sew around the top of the bag. Turn the bag through to the right side. Close the gap in the lining by hand or machine. Turn the lining into the bag, but leave a ¼" 'faux binding' around the top for the bag. Pin carefully, making sure that the handles are pinned up out of the way. Topstitch the 'binding' in place, then stitch across the handles, only a scant ¼", to attach the handles to the binding and keep them upright.

Now go grab your very favourite notions, tools and gizmos and fill your caddy. You're going to make a wonderful partnership!

# ‘KEEPING IT CRAFTY’ CADDY

**Now let’s make the project using the patchwork techniques on pages 38–45.**

**BORO**

Use boro piecing for the outer pockets.

**IMPROV**

Use improv piecing on the outside of the caddy – behind the vinyl pocket.

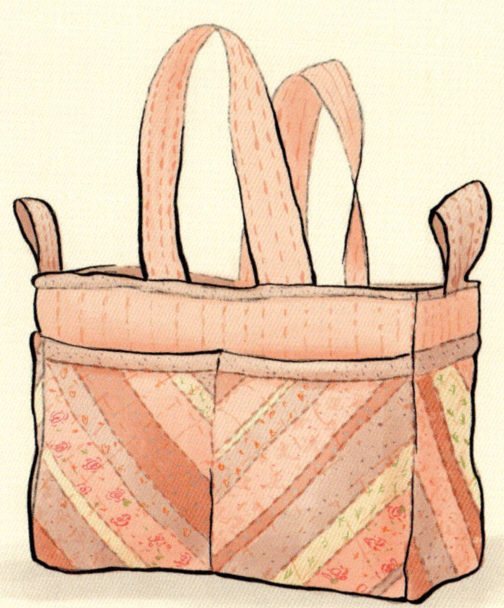

**STRING PIECE**

Create two panels of string piecing running in opposite directions … join them to create a ‘chevron’ effect.

**OPPOSITE: HEXI**

# KNITTING BAG

This is a really lovely simple-to-make bag, perfect for storing your latest knitting or crochet project in, and the circular handles and 'slip sides' allow good access to the bag's contents. It uses a pair of acrylic, plastic or wooden handles. You can sew the handles in by machine or hand sew if you prefer. Sewing by machine takes a certain amount of 'trust the process', but if you prefer hand sewing, go for it – just make sure your stitches are small, neat and you use nice, strong thread. I've used quilt-weight cotton for the outer and lining, and I've interfaced the outer fabric to give the bag soft structure. If you're using a slightly thicker fabric, omit the interfacing.

## FINISHED SIZE

12" x 11" (excluding handles), approx

## SKILL LEVEL

Confident beginner

## SKILLS USED

This is a very straightforward bag to sew, with easy side seams and very basic box corners. The construction technique can feel a little like fabric origami at first, but take your time and keep referring to the diagrams. You'll be sewing in a bag handle by machine, and it's a reasonably tight fit. But if you prefer, you can easily and very successfully sew the handle in by hand. Where there's a will!

**Gather your supplies! You will need...**

- Outer fabric (0.5m)
- Lining fabric (0.5m)
- Medium-weight fusible interfacing (optional) (0.5m)
- Thread to match your fabrics
- Pair of acrylic, plastic or wooden circular handles, 4½" diameter minimum
- Fabric-safe pen or pencil
- Pins

## LET'S MAKE THE BAG!

1 From each of the outer fabric, lining fabric and interfacing cut one 34" x 17" rectangle. If your fabric is directional, make sure the pattern is orientated 'portrait'. Fuse the interfacing to the wrong side of the outer fabric (you really only need to use this if the fabric is very light, like a cotton lawn).

2 ↓ Layer the outer and lining fabrics right sides together. Sew both short sides using a ¼" seam allowance. Open the fabrics up, then align both side seam allowances in the centre – the lining fabric should be right sides together and the outer fabric should also be right sides together with a folded edge at either end. Pin the raw edges together. Position double pins 5" down from the centre seam on both sides of the outer and lining fabrics.

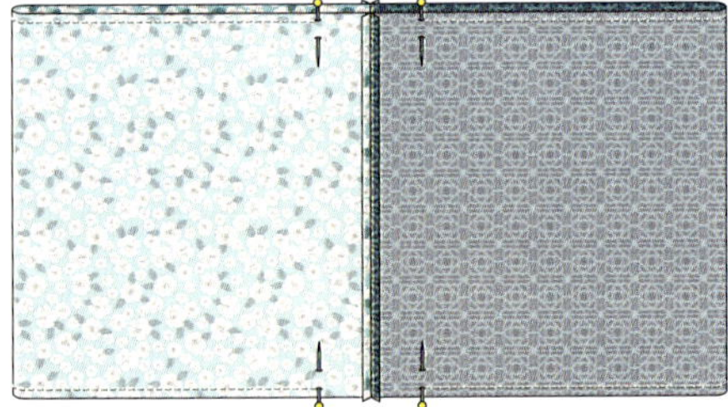

3 Sew four seams at the sides. Start at the double pin on one lining side and sew down to the corner. Repeat this on all four sides. This leaves a 10" gap on either side of the bag.

4 ↓ Mark 1½" squares at all four corners and cut these squares away.

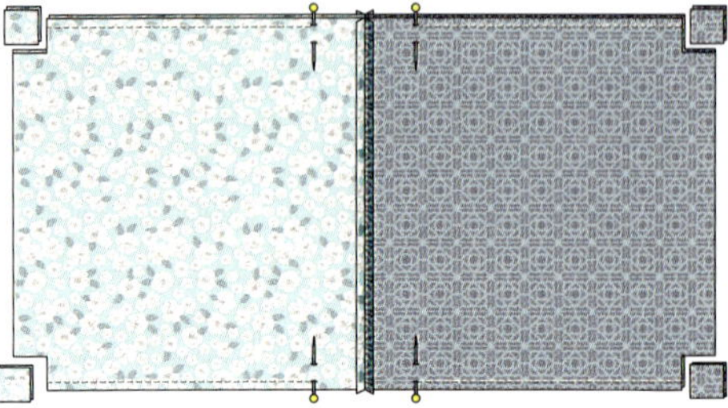

5 ↓ Box the corners.

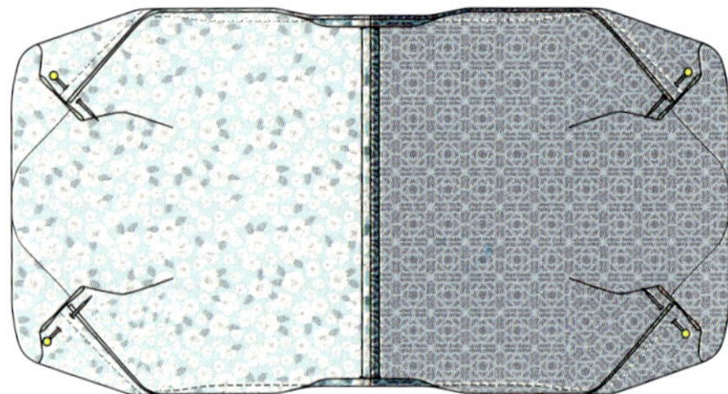

6 Fold the seam allowance in on the raw open edges by ¼" and press.

7 ↓ Bring the boxed corner of the outer and corresponding lining together on one side, matching the raw edges, and sew together ⅛" in from the raw edges. Repeat with the other two boxed corners.

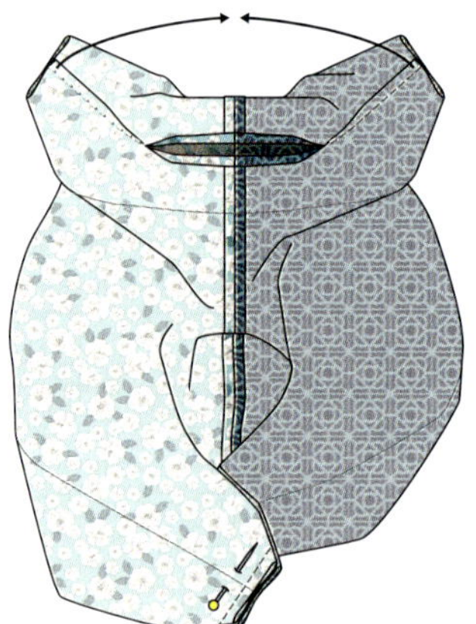

8 ↓ Turn the bag right sides out through the gap in the side. Bring the neatened but still open edges of the outer and lining together, forming an open 'V' shape at the sides of the bag. Pin very carefully, then sew around this 'V' close to the pressed edges to close and neaten.

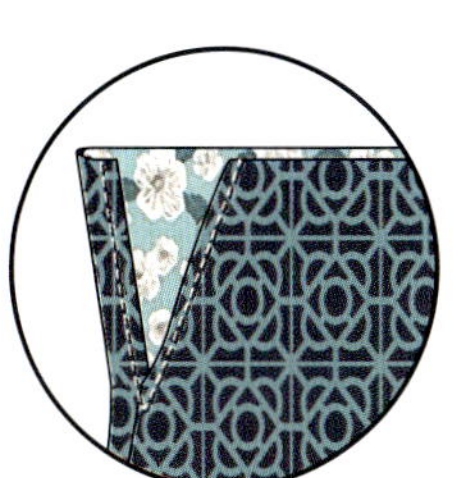

9 ↓ Mark a line 3" down from the top edges on the inside lining of the bag. This is the line you will turn the upper edge to when you add the handles.

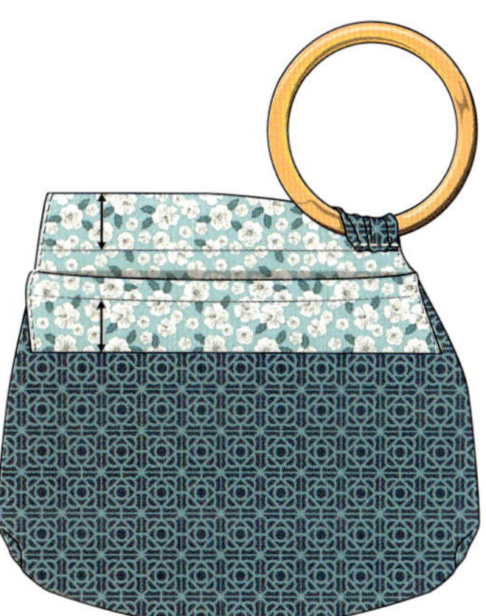

10 With the lining uppermost and starting with the circular handle at the right-hand side, fold the top edge of the handle through the ring and down until it meets the 3" line. Sew the top edge of the bag to this line by hand or machine. Allow the fabric to gather up over the handle as you go and make sure you reinforce the stitching at the start and end. Repeat with remaining handle.

# KNITTING BAG

**Now let's make the project using the patchwork techniques on pages 38–45.**

**BORO**

Create a boro panel for the lower part of the bag. Using plain fabric for the bag top makes it easier to gather into the handle.

**IMPROV**

Create improv quilting in narrow bands and join to make the bag.

**STRING PIECE**

Make string pieced blocks and join to make the main body of the bag.

**OPPOSITE: HEXI**

# 'SUN'S OUT!' GLASSES CASE AND LANYARD

Whether you use it for your sunglasses, your readers or even to carry your rotary cutter around at class, my 'sun's out' case with lanyard is a very useful little bag and a lot of fun to make. You can make it slightly wider or deeper to accommodate large sunnies: ½" to ¾" extra is enough. As an option, you can attach a D ring or triangular ring to the glasses case and make the lanyard too – I recommend it! You could also attach these to the lanyard, so make a few in your favourite fabrics. These are great for gifting too!

## FINISHED SIZE

4¼" x 6¾"

## SKILL LEVEL

Beginner

## SKILLS USED

You'll use Bosal In-R-Form foam, do some quilting, make a tab/loop and make a shoulder/neck strap.

**Gather your supplies! You will need...**

- Outer fabric and lining fabric 7½" x 9½" (landscape)
- 3" x 4" for the tab/loop (landscape)
- Fusible foam (7" x 9")
- One 1" D ring or triangular ring

**For the lanyard**

- Outer fabric (3" x 42")
- One ¾" swivel clasp
- Threads to match your fabrics
- Fabric-safe pen or pencil
- Pattern piece for the sunglasses case (see pullout template sheet)

## LET'S MAKE THE BAG!

1 ↓ Use the pattern piece to cut one outer fabric and one lining. Make sure you place the two fabrics right sides together and then cut out both pieces at once, ensuring a left- and right-facing curved edge.

2 Trim the ¼" seam allowance from the paper template, then cut one piece from Bosal In-R-Form, thus making it ¼" smaller on all sides. Fuse the foam to the wrong side of the outer piece.

3 ↓ Draw quilting lines on the outer fabric using the fabric-safe pen, then quilt as desired. I quilted diagonal lines ½" apart.

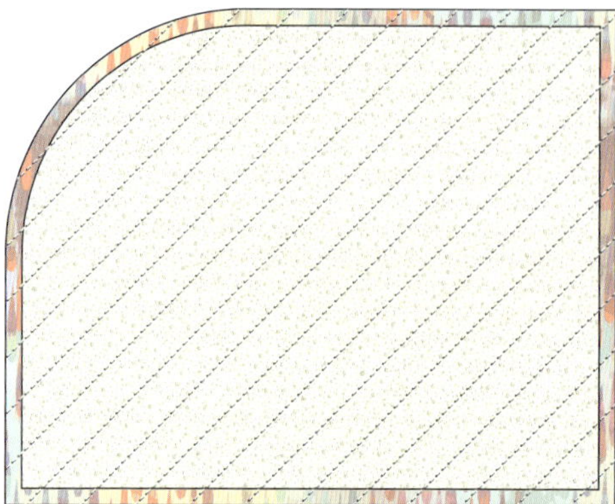

4 ↓ Make the tab/loop. Fold the 3" x 4" piece of fabric in half lengthways. Open it out, then fold the raw edges in to meet the centre crease. Press, then refold down the original crease to make a folded 3" x 1" strip and topstitch down both long edges.

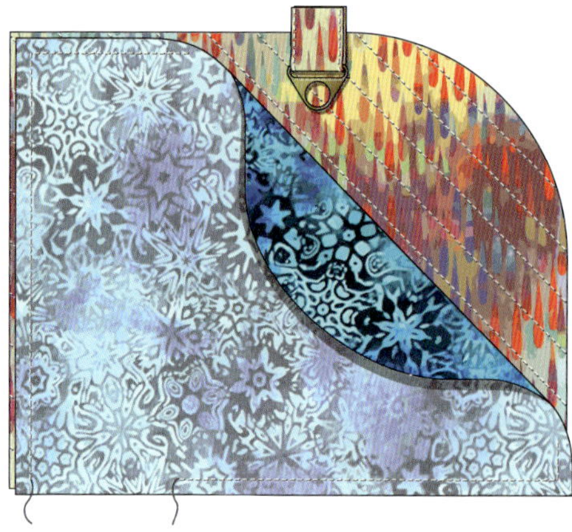

5 Thread the tab through the D ring/triangular ring and baste the raw edges together. Position this tab on the right side of the outer, as marked on the pattern, and baste in place.

6 Place the lining fabric on top of the outer, right sides together with the tab and ring inside. Pin around the whole perimeter, then sew around the perimeter using a ¼″ seam allowance. Leave a 2″ turning gap in the bottom edge.

7 ↓ Clip the corners and notch the curved seam allowance. Turn to the right side and press, then slipstitch the opening closed.

8 ↓ With the outer fabric outermost, fold the glasses case in half and line up the side and base seams. Sew across the top of the case, down the side and across the bottom (I did this twice for extra strength).

**Make the lanyard**

9 Fold the 3″ x 42″ strip in half lengthways, then press. Open out and turn the raw edges in, press again and refold to make a ¾″ wide strip. Topstitch both long edges.

10 Thread the shoulder/neck strap through the swivel clip, then overlap the raw ends by 1″. Sew. Now fold the raw edges under to neaten and sew a box around the turned edges to enclose them.

Clip the lanyard to your sunglasses case, pop in your sunnies and let's go ... the beach is waiting!

Time Out
Amst

# 'SUN'S OUT!' GLASSES CASE AND LANYARD

**Now let's make the project using the patchwork techniques on pages 38–45.**

**BORO**

Make sure you quilt your boro really well for this project. This is a 'high traffic' item and needs to be strong.

**IMPROV**

Use block fragments and scraps to create the outer bag.

**HEXI**

Hexi piece the outer panel – it's a great opportunity to use fussy-cut motifs.

**OPPOSITE: STRING PIECE**

# 'YOU CAN TAKE ME ANYWHERE' BAG

I love a bag you can take anywhere, and this is it: two big outer pockets designed for ease of access, a roomy interior that's fuss-free but includes a handy swivel clip to attach your keys to, an adjustable and detachable shoulder strap for all-day comfort, and it's a joy to sew too! The large outer pockets are the perfect place to showcase a fussy-cut fabric motif, machine embroidery or patchwork piecing, while the quilt binding edge creates a robust finish to the pocket and a natural break before the quilted outer bag. The bag has a secure zipped top, and I've used a chunky #5 zip to really draw attention to the metalware. If you can make a zipped pouch you can make this bag!

## FINISHED SIZE

13″ x 13″ x 3″

## SKILL LEVEL

Confident beginner

## SKILLS USED

Beginners, this is your bag to progress onto once you've mastered simple zippered pouches. There are a few more processes, but each one is easy – just take your time and build your bag. There are lots of layers in this bag, so it's essential that you keep seam allowances free of foam and interfacing. If you do that, then the bag is an easy sew and your sewing machine (and needles) will love you for it! You'll use paper pattern pieces, interfacing and fusible foam, do some quilting, bind an edge 'quilt style', make a lining, sew darts, make zip ends, insert a zip and make an adjustable shoulder strap. I know it sounds a lot for a beginner project, but this is the space between beginner and intermediate levels and it's so worth taking the leap!

**Gather your supplies! You will need...**

- Outer fabric A (0.5m)

**For the outer pockets**

(I've been generous because you might want to fussy-cut your fabrics, as I did. Some motifs on fabric are placed weirdly and you might need more, so check before you start cutting)

- Outer fabric B (0.5m)

**For the main body of the bag, front and back**

(I chose something low key but gorgeous so that the pocket fabric could really pop)

- A fat eighth of an accent print, fabric C

**For the pocket bindings and zip ends**

(I used a strip because a stripy binding almost always looks better than a non-stripy version)

- Lining fabric (0.5m)

**For lining the pockets and main body**

(you'll probably never see the linings of the pockets, so don't waste something really awesome)

- 10″ #5 zip and #5 zip pull (you can substitute a regular 10″ zip if you prefer)

*Continues overleaf*

## LET'S MAKE THE BAG!

1 First things first: are you right- or left-handed? Which side do you carry your bag? Because you'll want the outer pockets orientated in such a way that you can just slip your hand inside without too much thought. Just flip the pocket pattern piece to create a left or a right opening pocket.

2 ↓ From outer fabric A cut two pocket pieces. Layer these pocket pieces onto the fusible side of the interfacing, wrong side of the fabric facing down, and fuse lightly, avoiding the outer 1". Cut the interfacing out following the shape of the pocket, then lift the interfacing away from the edge of the fabric and trim a generous ¼" off all sides, except the curved inner edge of the pocket – we want the interfacing right up to the edge of the fabric here. Repeat on the second pocket.

*Continues overleaf*

- Two 1" aperture triangular rings or D rings
- Three 1" aperture lobster/swivel clasps
- One 1" aperture strap slider
- 60" of 1" webbing, for the shoulder strap
- Threads to match your fabrics
- Bosal single-side fusible foam
- Fabric-safe pen or pencil
- Medium-weight fusible interfacing
- Pattern pieces (see pullout template sheet)

3 Use the same pocket template to cut two mirror-image pockets from the lining fabric. Pin a lining to a pocket, right sides facing out and matching all raw edges. Baste the pocket and pocket lining together within the ¼" seam allowance. Bring the cut edges of the darts together and sew the darts using a ¼" seam allowance. Once you have sewn the darts, zigzag the raw edges to neaten them. Make two.

4 ↓ From accent fabric C cut two 2½" x 12" strips and fold each in half lengthways, wrong sides together, and press to make two binding strips. Use the strips to bind the inner curved edge of the pockets, sewing first from the front to attach the binding.

5 Clip little notches into the seam allowance to help the fabric to bend. Now flip the folded edge to the lining side of the pocket and either sew in place by hand or sew from the front again 'in the ditch' to catch the back fold. Trim the ends of the binding with the edge of the pocket. Make two.

6 ↓ Use the pattern piece for the main body of the bag. From outer fabric B cut two panels: one for the front of the bag and one for the back. Lightly fuse the shapes to the fusible side of the Bosal foam – as before, just lightly fuse the shape, avoiding the outer 1". Trim the foam back to the fabric edge first, then trim a further generous ¼" of foam away so that there is none in the seam allowance.

7 Mark and quilt the bag front and back. I marked a 1½" crosshatch using a fabric-safe pen. Remove the markings and then sew the darts as before. There is no need to zigzag the raw edges this time.

8 ↓ Place one pocket over the bag front and align the raw edges. Baste the pocket to the bag front. Repeat with the bag back and the remaining pocket.

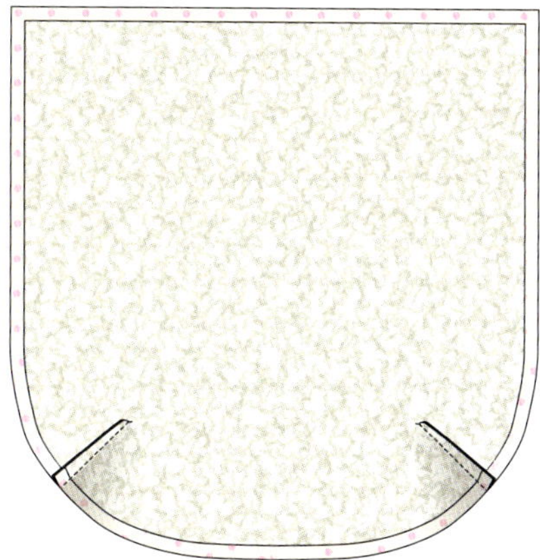

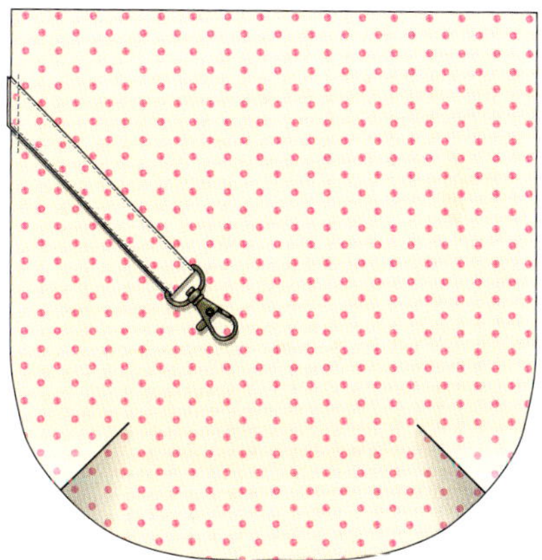

9 Make the zip ends. From accent fabric C cut two 2″ x 4″ rectangles and turn under ¼″ on either short end. Press, then press the whole strip in half so that the folded ends cover each other. Make two.

10 Slip these zip ends over the ends of the zip and topstitch neatly in place. Trim the sides of the zip ends to line up with the zipper tape. Measure the zip and trim evenly to 13½″.

11 → Make the lining. Use the main front and back pattern piece and cut out two lining pieces. Interface both lining pieces, trimming the interfacing a generous ¼″ from the raw edges of the fabric on all sides. Cut one 4″ x 8″ rectangle of lining fabric. Fold and press down the centre line, fold the raw edges in to meet the centre line, then refold to create a 1″ folded-flap strap, then topstitch both long edges. Slip this tab through one of the lobster clasps. Position the tab about 2″ down from the top edge of one lining piece, in the side seam, then baste in place.

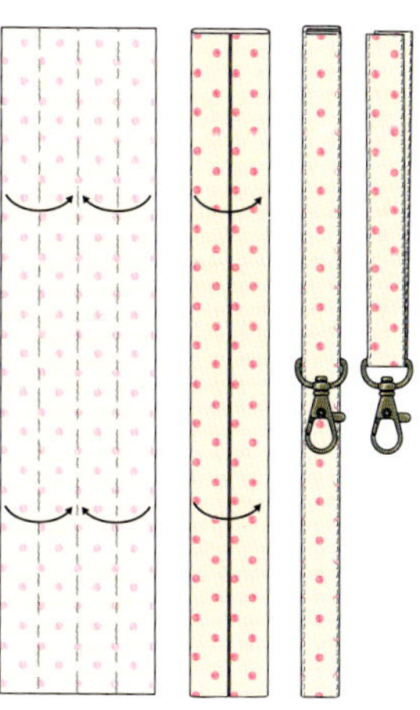

*Continues overleaf*

**12** Make the darts in the lining pieces.

**13** ↓ Insert the zip. Follow the instructions on page 28. Layer the zip onto the bag front, right sides touching and raw edges aligned. Layer the lining on top and pin carefully. Using a zipper foot, sew the top seam, attaching the zip to the bag front and lining. Flip the fabrics open, then bring the outer and lining together, wrong sides touching. Press, then topstitch close to the zipper, again using a zipper foot.

**14** Repeat this process on the other side of the zipper with the bag back and the second lining piece.

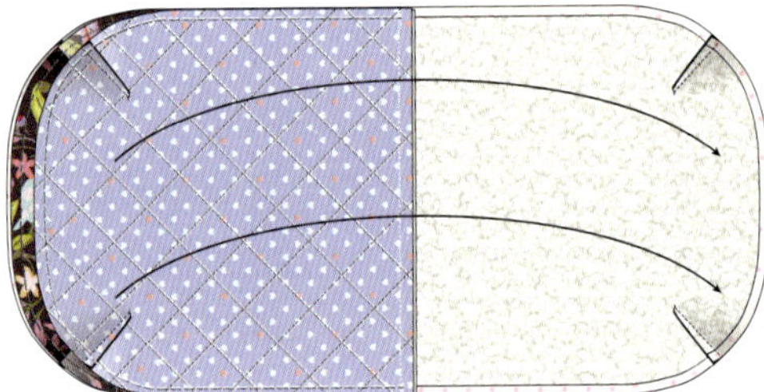

**15** ↓ Make the triangular or D ring attachments. Cut one 4" x 8" piece of outer fabric B. Fold in half lengthways, wrong sides together, and press. Open out and press the raw edges to the centre. Finally, refold, press and topstitch.

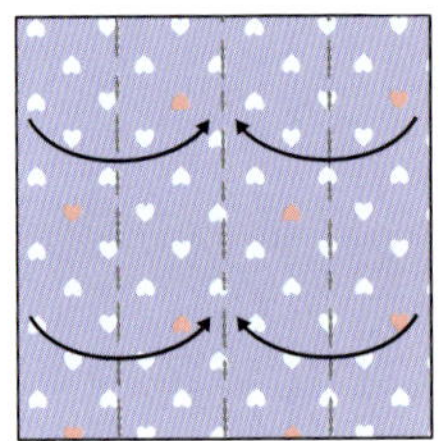

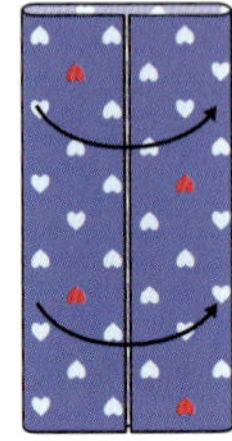

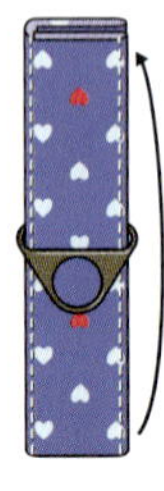

**16** ↓ Cut the tab in half to make two 4" lengths and thread each through a triangular or D ring. Baste these attachments to the top front of the bag, ¾" down from the top edge.

**17** ↓ Make up the bag! With the zipper fully opened, bring the bag front and back together, right sides touching; and the front and back lining, also right sides touching. Pin the lining to the lining and the outer to the outer. Sew all around the perimeter of the bag, leaving a generous 4" gap in the base of the lining. Turn the bag through to the right side, press and close the gap in the lining, by hand or machine.

**18** Close the zipper on the bag.

**19** Use the webbing and the two lobster clasps to make an adjustable shoulder strap following general instructions (see page 32). Attach the strap to your fabulous bag and try it on for size!

**20** If you like the idea of using webbing for a shoulder strap but want to make it a little more matched to your bag, take a 1" x 60" strip of fabric and pass it through a ½" bias tape maker to create a ½" wide folded strip. Carefully topstitch this fabric strip down the centre of the webbing and then proceed to make up the adjustable shoulder strap as before.

Now you can literally go anywhere!

# 'YOU CAN TAKE ME ANYWHERE' BAG

**Now let's make the project using the patchwork techniques on pages 38–45.**

**HEXI**

Large hexis look great on the outer pocket.

**IMPROV**

Use a combination of half square and half rectangle triangles, strips and squares.

**STRING PIECE**

Create a centre band of string piecing, trim the edges clean and then add further strings to both sides.

**OPPOSITE: BORO**

# THE BINDLE BAG

I named this bag 'The Bindle' after the sticks used by travellers in Australia. It's a great alternative to the hobo bag and a much easier make. You'll have this one done in no time and it's comfy to wear and roomy too. There's a zippered pocket inside and a magnetic snap fastening for security.

## FINISHED SIZE

14″ x 10″ x 5″

## SKILL LEVEL

Beginner

## SKILLS USED

You'll use a paper pattern, use interfacing, make darts, sew a letterbox zip, make a lining, add a magnetic snap and do some topstitching.

I used a heavy-weight tapestry fabric for the outer bag, which means I don't need to use any interfacing. If you are using a quilt-weight cotton or a softer denim, then use a medium-weight fusible interfacing, or you could softly pad the bag using H640 fusible fleece as your interfacing. I used cotton webbing for the handles, but you could make shoulder straps from fabric if you prefer: use 2″ wide strips of fabric, interfaced and sewn together to make a 1½″ finished shoulder strap.

**Gather your supplies! You will need...**

- Fabric A (0.5m)
  For the outside of the bag (cut 2 main pattern pieces, transferring darts and notches)

- Fabric B (0.5m)

**For the lining**
(cut 2 main pattern pieces, transferring darts and notches)

- Fat quarter of fabric C

**For the inside zippered pocket**
(cut two 9″ squares)

- One 7″ zip

- 1½″ wide cotton webbing for the shoulder straps (1m cut into two 16″ lengths)

- Threads to match your fabrics

  Fusible interfacing (enough to interface the outer bag pieces if you are using a light cotton. Whatever your fabric choices, you will need two 2″ squares of fusible interfacing to reinforce the magnetic snap)

  Magnetic Snap

- Pattern pieces for the outer bag and pocket (see pullout template sheet)

## LET'S MAKE THE BAG!

1 ↓ Use the paper pattern piece (see pullout template sheet) to cut out two fabric A (bag) pieces and two fabric B (lining) pieces. Transfer the darts and the notches to the wrong side of the fabrics. Also mark the position of the magnetic snap on the lining pieces only, and fuse the 2" squares of interfacing over this point on the wrong side of the lining.

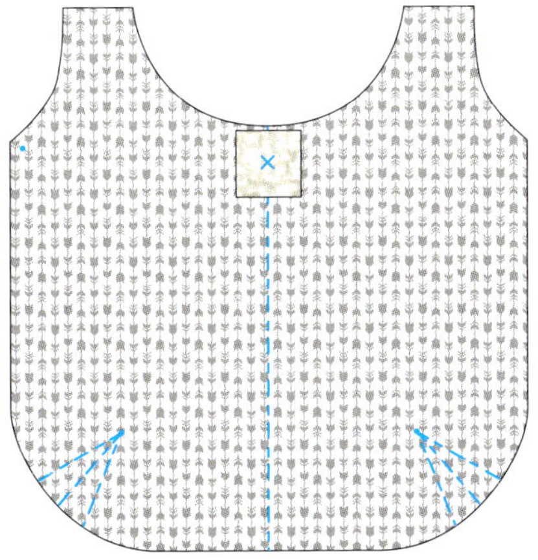

2 ↓ Make the letterbox zip. On the wrong side of one of the 9" squares of pocket fabric, mark a rectangle 1½" down from the top edge. The rectangle should be ½" wide and 7" in length, set in 1" from each side. Layer the marked square, right side to right side, with one of the lining pieces 2" down from the top edge. Pin the square in place, then sew around the rectangle using a slightly shorter stitch and following the marked line exactly.

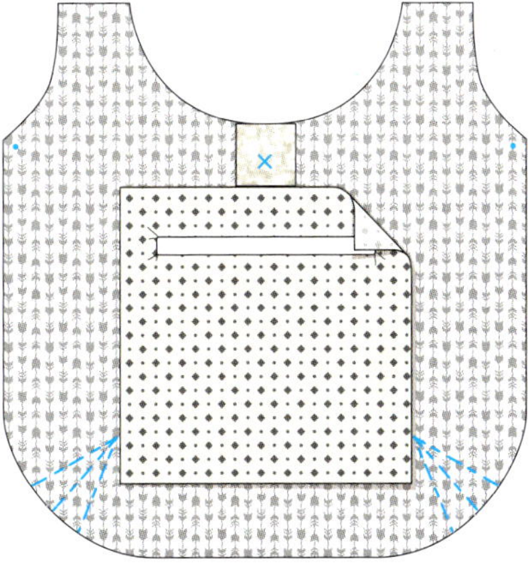

3 Cut down the centre of the rectangle and out to the corners. Turn the square through to the wrong side of the bag lining and press the letterbox opening neatly. Set and pin the zip behind the letterbox opening and sew in place using a zipper foot.

4 Take the second 9" square of pocket fabric and place it right sides together with the one already sewn into the lining. Pin the two pocket pieces together, then sew all around the pocket squares only.

5 Sew the darts on both lining pieces. Do this by folding the dart down the centre line, matching the two outer lines together. Sew from the wide end of the dart to the point. Press the darts neatly.

*Continues overleaf*

6 ↓ Install the two halves of the magnetic snap in the marked position. Set the lining pieces aside for now.

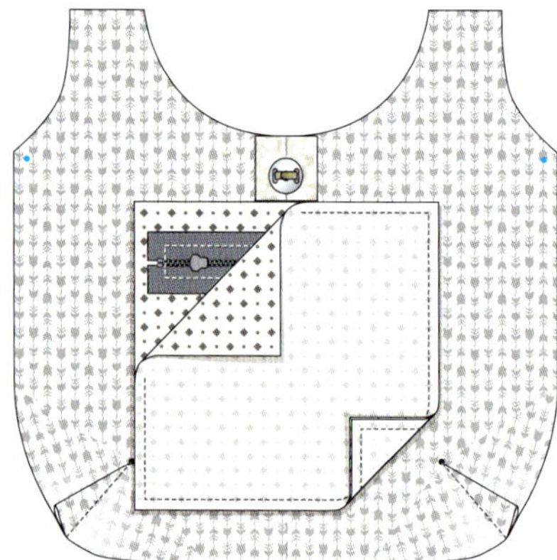

7 ↓ Make the outer bag. Make the darts as before and press. Baste the handles in place at the top of both bag pieces. Make sure the handles sit within the seam allowance and allow ¼" of the handle to overhang the fabric. Baste securely and make sure you don't twist the handles.

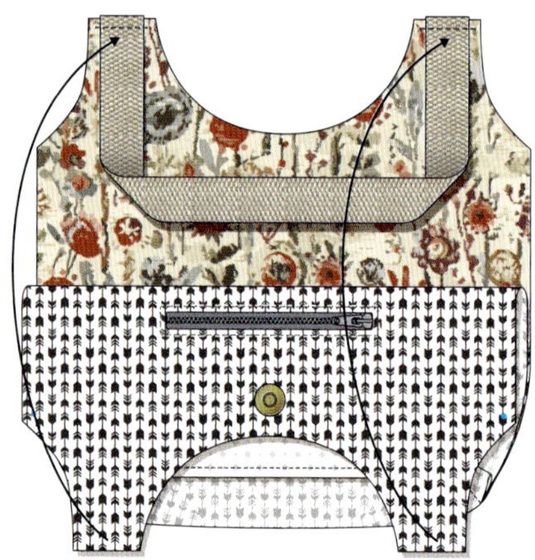

8 ↓ With the handles hanging down, layer one outer and one lining piece right sides together. Sew from marked point at outer left edge to marked point at outer right edge, backstitching at the start and finish. Pull the handles through gently, but leave the bag inside out for now. Repeat with the second outer and lining piece.

9 ↓ Place the two halves of the bag right sides together, outer to outer and lining to lining. Match up the darts, centre the bottom notches, centre the top notch and pin well. Leave the bottom open and the lining unpinned for a turning gap.

10 ↓ Start by sewing the lining. Sew from the original start point round to the original end point on the lining only.

11 ↓ Now sew the outer bag from the start point to the end point, backstitching at the start and finish.

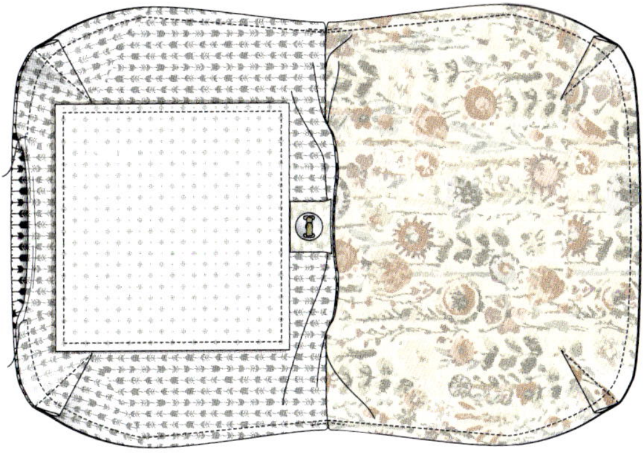

12 Turn the bag to the right side through the gap in the lining. Press well, then sew the gap in the lining by hand or machine.

13 Press around the top of the bag and topstitch ¼" in from the edge to finish. I've included an optional seam line on the main pattern piece; this is for the outer only and would be a great place to join two different fabrics – faux leather lower, cotton canvas upper; cork lower, oil cloth upper. Experiment with different fabrics, but remember, if you are using fabrics with very different weights or qualities, use interfacing to make them both feel and behave the same.

# THE BINDLE BAG

**Now let's make the project using the patchwork techniques on pages 38–45.**

## HEXI

Use a combo of large and tiny hexagons for the outer bag. Make three strips of patchwork, then trim the edges straight before joining.

## IMPROV

Create large-scale improv piecing to suit the size of the bag.

## STRING PIECE

Simply string piece this bag front and back.

**OPPOSITE: BORO**

# THE BOXING CLEVER POUCH

My boxing clever pouch might just become your new obsession make. You know that project you can't stop making, the one that looks great in any fabric and you can think of a hundred reasons to gift it to just about everyone you know?! Seriously, the boxing clever pouch is a fun one, and it's fast and easy to make. It has a super-smart exterior and a clean interior with no raw edges. It's a great size too and perfect for a washbag or as a make-up holdall. It's also ace for storing crafting and sewing supplies, pet grooming kits, gardening tools ... sorry, I'm obsessed with the usefulness of this one!

## FINISHED SIZE

9″ x 5½″ x 4½″

## SKILL LEVEL

Beginner

## SKILLS USED

The level is pretty easy. You'll do some quilting, use an interfacing, sew in a zip, make loops and sew simple box corners. Nothing tricky here, but a great project to move on to after you feel comfortable with the most basic of bag-making skills.

**Gather your supplies! You will need...**

- Two rectangles of outer fabric 10½″ x 14½″ (landscape)
- Two 10½″ x 14½″ rectangles of lining fabric
- One 2″ x 14″ strip of lining fabric (or outer, it's up to you) for the tab ends
- One 15″ or 16″ zip with zip pull (I used a #5 zip, but you could use a #3 zip too)
- Threads to match your fabrics
- Two 12″ x 16″ rectangles of regular quilt batting
- Two 10″ x 14″ rectangles of fusible interfacing and one ½″ x 14″ strip of interfacing
- Fabric-safe pen or pencil
- 505 quilt-basting spray or curved safety pins

## LET'S MAKE THE BAG!

1 Layer each of the rectangles of outer fabric with the pieces of batting (the batting is cut slightly larger on all sides), making sure the fabric is centred with a margin of batting all around. Fuse the two layers together with 505 quilt-basting spray, or pin with the curved safety pins. Mark the quilting lines with the fabric-safe pen, then quilt as desired. I quilted a 1½" diamond grid. When the quilting is completed, remove the markings and then trim the batting back to the edges of the fabric.

2 Fuse the large interfacing rectangles to the wrong side of the lining fabrics.

3 ↓ Take the 2" x 14" strip of lining fabric and fold it in half lengthways, wrong sides together, and press. Open out the fold and turn the raw outer edges in to meet the centre crease. Press again, then unfold: this divides the strip up into ¼" lengthways.

4 ↓ Now place the ½" strip of interfacing on one of the inner ½" wide divisions and press in place. Refold the strip and topstitch along both long edges. Cut the strap in half to make two ½" x 7" tab ends. Set aside.

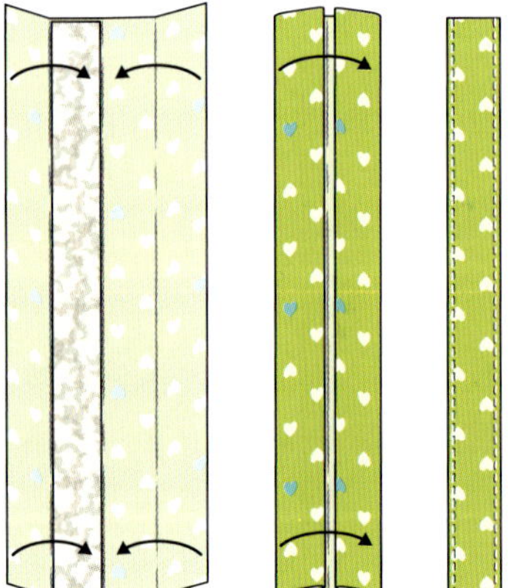

5 Sew the zip between the outer and lining pieces. Place one quilted outer bag piece, right sides facing, on the right side of the zip. Align the raw edges of the outer and the zip tape, then place the lining on the other side of the zip tape. Sew along the edge using a zip foot. Open out the outer and lining, press back and then together, and topstitch near the edge of the zip. Repeat on the other side of the zip with the remaining bag front and lining.

6 ↓ Open the bag out flat. Baste the tab ends to either side of the zip teeth. Place the ends of the tab ends side by side – do not overlap them. Open the zip at least halfway.

7 ↓ Fold the bag together so that the outer bag front and back are touching and the lining pieces are touching. Pin the bottom edges of the outers together and the linings together. Sew the outer bottom seam and the lining bottom seam, but leave a 4" turning gap in the centre of the lining bottom seam.

8 ↓ Press the bottom seams open. Now bring the outer bottom seam to meet the zipper teeth, folding the outer bag pieces in half, right sides touching. Do the same with the lining pieces: the outer and linings should be sitting one on top of the other, raw side edges lined up. Pin these edges together. Sew the side edges on both sides through all layers.

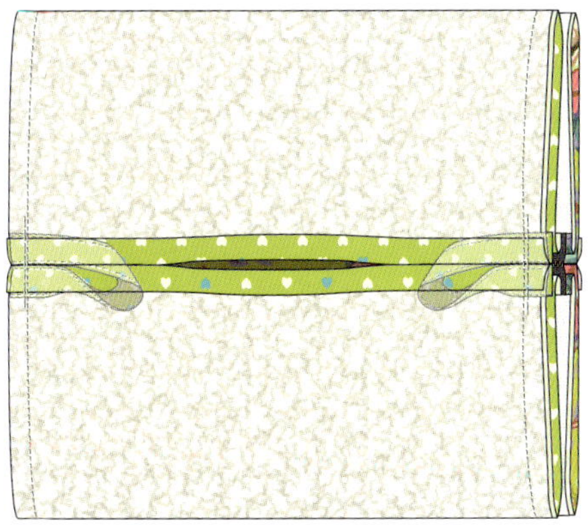

9 ↓ Turn the bag through to the right side. Push out the four corners and press flat with your iron. You should have a large rectangular flat pouch with a centre zip. It's all a bit weird and uninspiring at the moment, but trust the process!

10 ↓ Open the zip fully and turn the bag through to the lining side. Bring one of the side seams flat to meet the side of the bag, flattening the corner into a triangle and making sure the seam is centred – it's just like when you box a bag bottom! Press the corner triangle flat and pin. Repeat this on all four corners. Now using the fabric-safe pen, mark a line 2" down from the point of each triangle corner and draw a line straight across the tip of the triangle. Sew across the triangle corners on the marked lines. Turn the bag through to the right side and give it a gentle press.

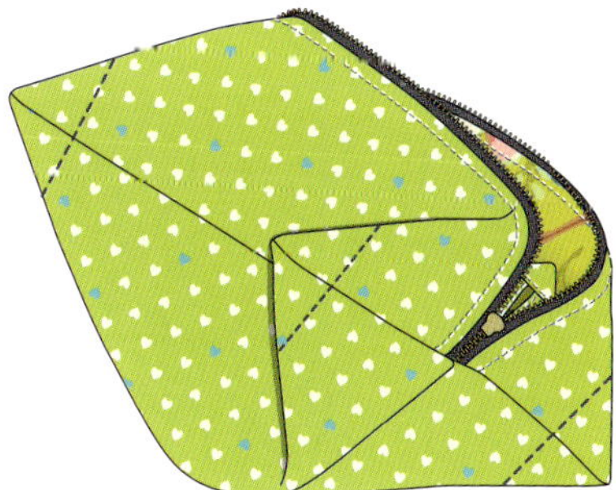

Do up the zip and admire your beautiful pouch. Now start planning your next and your next!

# THE BOXING CLEVER POUCH

**Now let's make the project using the patchwork techniques on pages 38–45.**

**BORO**

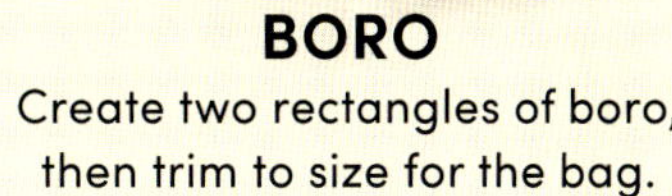

Create two rectangles of boro, then trim to size for the bag.

**IMPROV**

Use orphan blocks and 'log cabin' style piecing.

**STRING PIECE**

Use selvedges and scraps ... If your strips aren't long enough, join them with diagonal seams.

**OPPOSITE: HEXI**

# CASH OR CARD WALLET

My cash or card wallet is a quick and satisfying make: practical, smart and a lovely way to use up leftover scraps of fabric. It has a fastening flap that keeps both cash and credit cards secure, and the addition of a swivel clasp means you can clip it to the inside of a bag so you never lose your wallet!

## FINISHED SIZE

4½" x 3½"

## SKILL LEVEL

Confident beginner

## SKILLS USED

You'll make folded pockets, a fastening flap and add a swivel clasp. You'll also topstitch around thicker layers (a little daunting at first, maybe, but take your time, lengthen your stitch and use a walking foot ... easier than you thought!).

**Gather your supplies! You will need...**

- Fabric A (main fabric)
  One 5" x 7½" rectangle (portrait) for the main outer
  One 5" x 10" rectangle (portrait) for the lower credit card pocket
  One 2½" x 7" rectangle (portrait) for the fastening flap
- Fabric B (plain/solid/contrast)
  One 5" x 11½" rectangle (portrait) for the upper credit card pocket
  One 2" x 4" rectangle for the swivel clasp attachment
- Fabric C (lining)
  One 5" x 7½" rectangle (portrait)
  One 2½" x 7" rectangle for the fastening flap
- Medium-weight fusible interfacing
- Small round object to round off the corners of the fastening flap
- Heavy fusible interfacing 2" x 7"
- One ½" aperture swivel clasp
- One snap fastener/KAM snap and fixing tools, or sew-on popper
- Threads to match your fabrics

## LET'S MAKE THE WALLET!

1 Interface the main outer panel and the lining panel, the upper and lower credit card pockets and the swivel clip attaching strip with medium-weight fusible interfacing.

2 ↓ Take the upper credit card pocket piece and fold it in half, right sides together, matching the short ends. Sew together with a ¼″ seam allowance. Turn through to the right side, centre the seam allowance and press. Repeat with the lower credit card pocket.

3 ↓ Topstitch both credit card pockets along both short edges to finish neatly.

4 → Layer the upper and then the lower credit card pockets onto the outer main panel, and pin, then baste in place.

5 ↓ Make the fastening flap. Round the bottom edge of the heavy-weight interfacing, the outer and the lining fabrics. Fuse the interfacing to the outer fabric, centring it and leaving a ¼″ seam allowance all around the fabric. Layer the interfaced outer with the lining fabric, right sides together. Sew around the long edges and the curved lower edge, leaving the top open for turning. Turn and press. Topstitch all sides a scant ¼″ from the edge.

6 Sew the flap into place on the main outer panel. Find the centre of the main outer panel and place the flap, right side facing, with the raw edge of the flap lined up with the centre of the outer panel. Sew across the bottom of the flap. Trim the raw edge of the flap close to the stitching, then fold the flap up and over the first line of stitching and pin in place, but do not sew at this stage.

7 ↓ Make the swivel clasp attachment. Take the 2″ x 4″ strip of fabric B and fold it in half lengthways, wrong sides together, and press. Open out and fold the long raw edges in to meet the centre fold and press again, then refold the fabric down the original fold and press again. Topstitch down each long side. Slip the folded strip through the swivel clasp and baste the raw end together. Place the swivel clasp on the front left of the main outer wallet, aligning the top of the attachment to the top of the lower credit card pocket. Baste in place.

8 ↓ Fold the wallet in half, right sides together, and pin the side seams. Sew the side seams with a ¼″ seam allowance. Trim the seam allowance back to ⅛″ and turn to the right side. Press.

9 Make the lining by folding the interfaced lining piece in half, right sides together, and sewing the side seams using a ¼″ seam allowance. Leave a 2″ gap in one side of the turning. Trim the seam allowances as before.

10 Slip the outer wallet into the lining so that the right sides are touching. Match and pin around the top. Sew around the top of the bag using a ¼″ seam allowance. Turn to the right side. Hand sew the opening in the lining closed and push the lining into the wallet. Press.

11 ↓ Topstitch around the top of the wallet.

12 ↓ With the fastening flap still pinned upwards, covering the raw edge at the base, topstitch around the sides and base of the wallet, thus enclosing the raw edges of the flap.

13 Use the KAM snap fixing tools to apply a snap fastener to the flap and to the corresponding credit card pocket.

credit

# CASH OR CARD WALLET

**Now let's make the project using the patchwork techniques on pages 38–45.**

**BORO**

Use boro on the flap – keep your patches and stitches small and proportionate.

**IMPROV**

Adding improv piecing to the flap only will create lots of impact with little extra work.

**HEXI**

Use small hexis on the flap only – lovely style without adding bulk to the side seams.

OPPOSITE: **STRING PIECE**

# THE 'DASH' WALLET

This is the perfect bag when you are dashing to the shops in a hurry – you just need keys and your cash or credit card – or maybe an hour at the beach and you just need sun block and your sunnies. Wherever you're dashing to, make sure you have the 'dash' wallet with you!

## FINISHED SIZE

7″ x 5½″ x ¼″

## SKILL LEVEL

Intermediate

## SKILLS USED

You'll be fussy cutting fabric, inserting two zips, using lobster/swivel clasps, working with interfacing and sewing several heavy layers.

**Gather your supplies! You will need...**

- Two ½″ lobster/swivel clasps in your choice of finish
- Two 7″ nylon zips in toning or contrast colours
- 0.25m medium-weight fusible interfacing

**Outer fabrics:**

- One 5½″ x 5″ piece of fussy-cut feature fabric (landscape) for the front pocket (rabbit print)
- 1½″ x 18″ strip of contrast/toning fabric for the bag front (you may need more fabric if you are using a directional print), cut into two 1½″ x 5″ strips (portrait) and one 1½″ x 7½″ strip (landscape) (gold metallic chain print)
- Two 7½″ x 6″ rectangles (landscape) for the bag back and outer pocket lining (hexagon print)
- Lining fabric (neon mini polka dot print)
  Two 7½″ x 6″ rectangles for the bag lining
  One 7½″ x 5″ rectangle to line the lower part of the front zip pocket
  One 1½″ x 7½″ strip to line the upper part of the front zip pocket
  Two 1″ x 3″ rectangles for the zip ends
  One 2″ x 7″ rectangle for the lobster/swivel clasp loops

## LET'S MAKE THE BAG!

1 ↓ Start by making the outer zip pocket. Sew the 1½" x 5" rectangles of contrast fabric to either side of the fussy-cut pocket piece. Press the seams towards the narrow strips, then topstitch near the seams. The pocket piece should measure 5" x 7½". Interface the wrong side of the pocket piece.

2 Take one of the zips, the lower outer pocket piece made in step one and the 7½" x 5" piece of lining fabric and sew the lower half of the outer zip pocket and the corresponding lining piece to the zip. Press back and topstitch. Do the same thing with the 1½" x 7½" upper pocket piece and corresponding lining.

3 ↓ Sew to the zipper and then press back and topstitch as before. Trim the outer zip pocket carefully to 7½" x 6".

4 Make the lobster/swivel clasp loops. Take the 2" x 7" strip of lining fabric and fold down the centre and press, wrong sides together. Open out, then refold the raw edges in to meet at the centre crease and press again. Now refold down the original centre fold, encasing the raw edges, and press. Topstitch very close to both long edges.

5 Cut the strap in half to make two 3½" pieces. Insert one into the ring end of a lobster clasp, bring the raw edges of the loop together and baste. Make two. Set aside.

6 Make the outer bag. Interface both 7½" x 6" rectangles and machine baste the outer zip pocket to one of the interfaced rectangles, both right sides facing up. When you open up the zip you should see pretty fabric through the gap!

7 Make the main zip. This zip has tab ends. Take the two 1" x 3" zip tab pieces and the second zip. Take one zip end and place it wrong side up on a pressing surface. Fold ¼" in on both short ends and press, then fold the whole zip end in half, wrong sides together, matching the neatened ends and press. Make two.

8 ↓ Wrap one of the zip ends around the stopper end of the zip. Match the neatened ends, then topstitch through all layers to secure. Snip open the folded end of the zip tab and trim the excess zip tape away. Measure the zip to approximately 7" and trim the 'pull' end. Attach the second zip end to the 'pull' end as before, then trim the whole zip to 7½".

**9** Take the front and back outer pieces and the corresponding lining pieces, plus the second zip. Sew the zip pocket bag front and lining to the second zip, making sure the zip pull starts the same end as the zip pocket. Sew, press back and topstitch. Do the same with the bag back and corresponding lining.

**10** ↓ Bring the lining carefully out of the way and baste the lobster/swivel clasps in place either side of the front top band.

**11** Now open the main zip almost fully and then open out the outer fabrics away from the lining fabrics. You want outer touching outer and lining touching lining. Pin carefully, then use a small round object to round the lower corners on the outer and lining fabrics, leaving an obvious gap in the bottom edge of the lining.

**12** ↓ Sew around the entire bag, leaving a gap in the lining for turning!

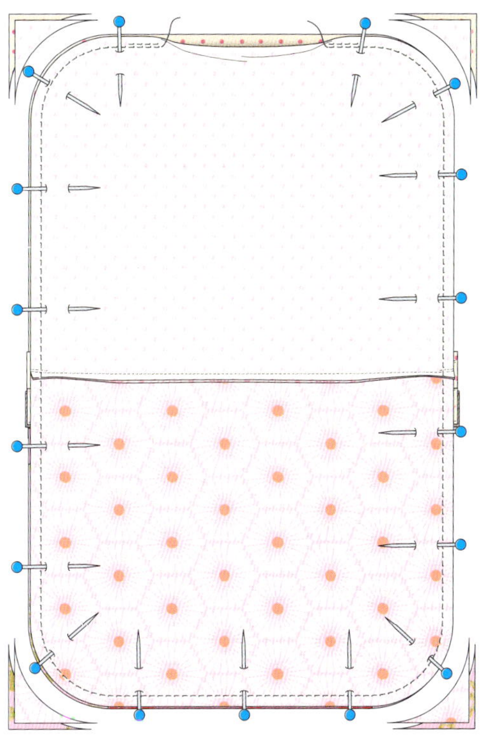

**13** Turn the bag through to the right sides and press neatly.

**14** Bring the lining out of the bag and match the edges of the lining. Slipstitch the opening closed.

**15** Turn the bag back through to the right side and give one last press.

Your 'dash' wallet is now complete. Let's go!

PWWM080 Chrysanthemum Tonal
PWWM008 Seaweed

# THE 'DASH' WALLET

**Now let's make the project using the patchwork techniques on pages 38–45.**

**BORO**
Substitute the fussy-cut centre panel with boro.

**IMPROV**
Improv piece 'wonky' geese for the front panel.

**HEXI**
Use small hexis to piece the centre panel.

**OPPOSITE: STRING PIECE**

# ESSENTIAL PURSE

My concertina-style purse is an essential make. It's perfect for your cash and cards, but also adaptable enough to use for storing a rotary cutter and scissors, plus a sewing kit for crafting on the go. Add small D rings to the sides and attach a chain and this would make a rather elegant evening bag. This is a great purse to experiment with: it's so quick and easy you'll make a whole batch before you know it!

## FINISHED SIZE

6½" x 4½" x 1"

## SKILL LEVEL

Beginner

## SKILLS USED

This is a nice easy make. You'll be using fusible foam quilting and making a very easy concertina pocket. You'll also apply KAM snaps or a press stud.

**Gather your supplies! You will need...**

- Fabric A for the main outer panel
  One 12" x 7" rectangle (portrait)
- Fabric B for the front pocket
  One 4" x 10" rectangle (landscape)
- Fabric C for the lining
  One 12" x 7" rectangle
  One 4" x 10" rectangle
- Bosal In-R-Form or fusible foam (single sided)
  One 11½" x 6½" panel
  One 3½" x 9½" panel
- Threads to match your fabrics
- One KAM snap, plus fixing tools or a sew-on press stud
- Hand-sewing needle
- Fabric-safe pen or pencil
- Small round object for rounding corners

## LET'S MAKE THE PURSE!

1 Layer the main outer panel with fusible foam. The foam is cut ¼" smaller on all sides, so get it centred. Fuse to the wrong side of the fabric. Mark the quilting design using the fabric-safe pen, or freestyle! I quilted a 1" diamond crosshatch. Quilt the design through the two layers of outer fabric and foam. Use the round object to round out the lower corners of the panel – just do the lower end – this will form the flap of the purse.

2 ↓ Repeat the process with the outer pocket piece and the corresponding fusible foam. I quilted horizontal lines ¾" apart. You don't need to round the corners this time.

3 ↓ Layer the quilted main panel with the corresponding lining piece, right sides together, and pin. Sew around the outside edge, leaving a 3" gap in one side for turning. Trim the seam allowance back a little. Turn through to the right side and press. Neaten the open gap and pin carefully together. Topstitch around the entire outer panel ⅛" in from the edge to finish and also to close the turning gap. Repeat the process with the outer pocket piece and the corresponding lining piece.

4 With the main outer panel right side up, measure 1" up from the upper (straight corners) edge. Mark a placement line here using the fabric-safe pen. Centre the outer pocket piece, right sides also facing up on this placement line. If your fabric is directional, the top of the design needs to be on the placement line. Pin in place.

5 ↓ Sew the lower edge of the pocket to the main panel, starting and finishing your sewing ¼" in from the edge. Make sure to reinforce the stitching here too.

6 ↓ Fold the purse up, bringing the side of the pocket piece to meet the side of the main panel, folding the excess pocket inwards to form the concertina fold. Pin carefully. Sew along this edge, attaching the pocket to the side of the purse. Repeat on the other side of the purse.

7 You may like to add a few hand stitches to the very bottom of the concertina fold. It can be quite tricky to machine sew into a tight fold, but it's easier by hand!

8 Give the purse a good press to set the concertina folds at the side.

9 ↓ Find the very centre of the flap and place a dot ½" up from the centre lower edge. Apply the outer part of the KAM snap or press stud here. Find the corresponding point on the front pocket where the flap naturally sits and place a mark. Apply the other half of the snap here.

10 Press the snap together with a reassuring click and you are done! You could substitute a magnetic snap for the KAM snap or press stud if you prefer.

Gütermann
OLFA

# ESSENTIAL PURSE

**Now let's make the project using the patchwork techniques on pages 38–45.**

**BORO**

Add boro to this purse but be sure to hand quilt densely to protect 'high traffic' areas.

**HEXI**

1" hexis look great used on both the the top and lower half of this purse.

**STRING PIECE**

String piece in one direction and then add further strips in the opposite direction.

OPPOSITE: **IMPROV**

# THE FAST AND FABULOUS TOTE

My fast and fabulous tote is destined to be a wardrobe staple. It's a quick and stylish make, perfect for showing off some favourite fabric or patchwork. It's roomy, secure and oh so stylish – and you won't believe how quickly it comes together!

## FINISHED SIZE

14″ x 11″ x 3″

## SKILL LEVEL

Beginner

## SKILLS USED

You'll use interfacing and fusible foam, do simple piecing, quilting and topstitching. There's an optional letterbox zippered pocket, and you'll use sew-on faux leather handles and a press stud fastening.

**Gather your supplies! You will need...**

- Main fabric for the outer bag central panels: fat quarter
- Two 8½″ x 17″ rectangles (landscape)

- Contrast fabric for the outer bag upper bands: fat eighth
  Two 3½″ x 17″ rectangles (landscape)

- Contrast fabric for the outer bag base panel: fat eighth
  One 5½″ x 17″ rectangle (landscape)

- Lining fabric for the upper facing: fat eighth
- Two 3½″ x 17″ rectangles (landscape)

- Main lining fabric: between 0.5m and 0.75m (depending if the fabric is directional)
  One 17″ x 21½″ rectangle (portrait if directional, otherwise cut landscape for economy)
  One inner pocket piece 10″ x 16″ (portrait if directional)

- Frixion or fabric-safe pen or pencil

- One pair of 24″ long faux leather sew-on handles

- One ¾″ (21mm) snap fastener

- Threads for piecing, quilting and hand sewing the snap and handles, plus appropriate needles

- One 8″ zip to match the lining fabric

- One 17″ x 27½″ piece of Bosal single-sided fusible foam

- 0.5m medium-weight fusible interfacing

- Pattern pieces (see pullout template sheet)

## LET'S MAKE THE BAG!

1 Arrange the outer bag pieces: upper band, middle band, base band, middle band (upside-down if the fabric is reversible), upper band (upside-down if the fabric is reversible). Sew the panels together using a ¼" seam allowance. Press carefully. The panel should measure 17" x 27½".

2 Fuse the pieced panel to the fusible foam and allow to cool completely. Mark your quilting design using a Frixion or fabric-safe pen (I marked a 2" diagonal crosshatch grid over the entire surface of my bag panel). Quilt the panel using your choice of thread and a walking foot. Remove the marked lines after quilting is complete.

3 ↓ Use the centre curve marking template (on the pullout sheet) to mark and cut away the upper portions of the bag outer. Repeat on both upper bands. Find the centre of the bag base and mark a line using a Frixion pen. Now mark a 1½" x 3" rectangle at either side of the bag base, centring it on this midway line. Trim this rectangle away.

4 ↓ Bring the right sides of the bag outer together, matching the side seams, and pin. Sew the side seams using a ¼" seam allowance. Bring the cut edges of the trimmed base rectangles together and sew across to 'box' the bottom of the bag. Turn the bag through to the right side and press the seams carefully. Set aside.

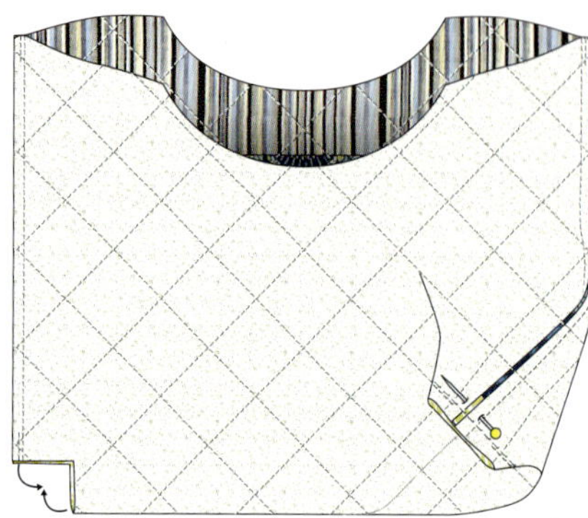

5 ↓ Make the lining. Arrange the upper facing pieces at the top and bottom of the main lining piece. Sew together using a generous ¼" seam allowance. Press, then topstitch near the upper facing seams. Interface the entire lining on the wrong side.

**Make an optional letterbox zippered pocket**

6 Interface the 10" x 16" pocket piece on the wrong side. On the wrong side of the pocket piece at the top of the rectangle (portrait), draw a straight line 1" down from the top of the rectangle, from side to side. Draw a second line ½" down from this first line. Now mark off the ends 1" in from the sides to create an 8" x ½" rectangle positioned 1" down from the top of the pocket piece.

7 Layer this marked rectangle onto the lining fabric, right sides together. Position the pocket centrally so that the upper raw edge of the pocket piece is level with the facing seam, then pin in place.

8 Sew around the marked rectangle, directly on the drawn line. Cut through the very centre of the rectangle up to ¼" from the ends, then snip out to the corners at right angles using very sharp pointed scissors.

9 Turn the pocket piece through to the wrong side of the bag lining. Carefully flatten out the 'letterbox' and press carefully. Position the zip behind the letterbox opening and baste in place, then machine sew around the zip using a zipper foot.

10 Fold up the lower half of the pocket piece to meet the upper raw edge and pin the side seams together. Sew the side seams using a ¼" seam allowance. Pin and sew the top edge of the pocket pieces together. Be sure to only sew pocket piece to pocket piece – you shouldn't be sewing through the main lining fabric!

11 Use the centre curve marking template to mark and cut away the upper portions of the bag lining. Repeat on both upper facings. Find the centre of the bag lining base and mark a line using a Frixion pen. Now mark a 1½" x 3" rectangle at either side of the bag base, centring it on this midway line. Trim these rectangles away.

12 Make the bag lining up in exactly the same way as the outer bag, save for two differences: use a generous ¼" seam allowance this time and leave a 4" to 5" gap unsewn in one of the lining sides for turning the bag through.

13 ↓ Place the outer bag into the lining, right sides together. Carefully pin the upper edges together, being careful not to stretch the curved edges. Sew around the top of the bag using a ¼" seam allowance. Turn the bag through to the right side and carefully press, paying particular attention to the curved edges.

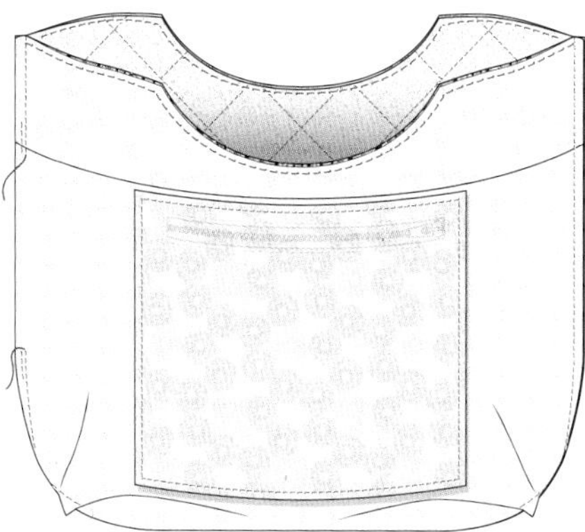

14 Pin the top edges of the bag, then topstitch around the entire top of the bag using a longer stitch (3.5).

15 Position the snap fastener centrally at the top of the lining approximately ½" down from the upper edge. Carefully mark a dot using a Frixion pen, then hand sew each half of the snap fastener using 3 or 4 stitches through each gap. Make sure you do this very securely!

16 Finally, position and sew the faux leather handles to the outer bag using double thread and a backstitch. I also like to add an 'X' at the top of the handle sometimes for extra durability.

# THE FAST AND FABULOUS TOTE

**Now let's make the project using the patchwork techniques on pages 38–45.**

### BORO

Focus the boro piecing on the centre bag panel. Stitch to a light fabric foundation before adding the top and base.

### IMPROV

Use patchwork scraps, selvedges and triangles to piece the centre portion of the bag.

### HEXI

Large hexis work well in the middle section of the bag – add a dash of extra colour with covered piping cord between the bands.

**OPPOSITE: STRING PIECE**

# THE 'IT'S A DATE' BAG

This is the perfect grab-and-go bag. It's roomy enough for all your essentials but small enough not to overwhelm! There's a fully zippered top and an additional zippered pocket on the front of the bag – it pays to be organised! It also offers great flexibility as it can be worn as a wristlet, an over-the-shoulder or a clutch. This might just be your new favourite!

## FINISHED SIZE

10″ x 8″ x 3″

## SKILL LEVEL

Intermediate

## SKILLS USED

You'll be making a box pouch, quilting, adding appliqué, inserting a regular zip and a letterbox zip, using lobster/swivel clasps, working with interfacing and sewing several heavy layers.

**Gather your supplies! You will need...**

- 0.5m feature fabric for the outside of the bag and shoulder strap
  Two 12″ x 13″ rectangles of outer feature fabric (landscape). You'll trim this down to 10½″ x 11½″ after quilting, so keep this in mind if you want to centre any motifs
  One strip 4″ x width of fabric (approx 42″) for the shoulder strap
  Two 12″ x 13″ pieces of quilting batting/wadding
  Two 12″ x 13″ pieces of lightweight cotton or quilters calico to back the quilted sandwich (this won't be seen in the finished bag)

- Frixion or fabric-safe pen or pencil

- 0.5m medium-weight fusible interfacing

- 0.5m contrast fabric for the bag lining, outer appliqués, tabs, zip ends, wristlet
  Two 10½″ x 11½″ rectangles (landscape) for the bag lining
  Four 4½″ squares for the outer appliqués
  Two 8″ squares for the zip pocket lining
  One 4″ x 25″ strip for the wristlet and D ring loops
  Two 1¼″ x 3″ rectangles for the zip ends

- Two #5 zips, one 8″ for the zippered pocket and one 10″ for the main bag zip

- Thread for quilting, appliqué and construction

*Continues overleaf*

## LET'S MAKE THE BAG!

1 Layer the outer fabric pieces with batting and calico backing. Baste with 505 spray or curved safety pins. Mark your quilting lines (I marked a 1″ diagonal grid).

2 Quilt the marked lines by hand or machine. I machine quilted using a longer stitch length (3.5) and a walking foot, which guides the layers smoothly. When the quilting is completed you can give your work a light press to remove the Frixion pen and then carefully trim the panels to 10½″ x 11½″ (landscape).

3 ↓ Use the 4″ quarter circle template (on the pullout template sheet) and trace onto the wrong side of each of the four 4½″ squares of contrast fabric for the appliqués. Cut four 4½″ squares of interfacing and place the fusible side against the right side of the fabric. Pin carefully. Sew on the curved line using a shorter than normal stitch (1.8). Trim the fabric and interfacing to within ⅛″ of the curved edge and along the drawn right angles. Turn the fabric through to the wrong side and carefully finger press only – don't use an iron! The fusible side of the interfacing should now be on the back of the quarter circle appliqués. Position them at the lower corners of the front and back quilted bag panels and fuse in place with a hot, dry iron. Sew the appliqués in place with a straight stitch (length 3.5), sewing very close to the curved edge and basting the raw straight edges.

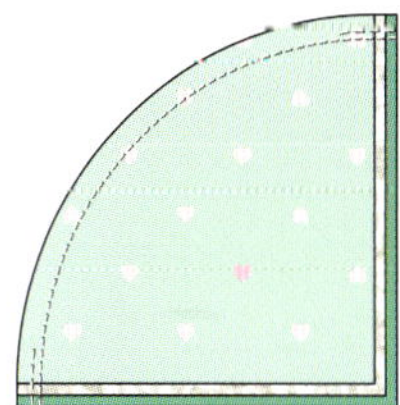

4 Interface both 8″ squares of zippered pocket lining fabric. On the wrong side of one of the squares mark a rectangle: measure 2″ down from the top of the square and draw a pencil line right across the square. Measure ½″ down from this

*Continues overleaf*

- Two 1″ D rings
- Three 20mm aperture lobster/swivel clasps
- 505 basting spray or curved safety pins
- Quilters double-sided ¼″ tape (optional)
- Pattern piece (see pullout template sheet)

line and draw a second line. Now measure ½" in from the edge of the square and draw a short line joining the two horizontals. Repeat on the other side of the square. You should now have a 7" long x ½" wide rectangle drawn on the back of the fabric piece, 2" down from the top edge.

5 Make the 'letterbox opening' for the zip. Layer this marked square on top of the front quilted panel of the main bag, centred, right sides together and tops aligned. Pin in place. Using a short stitch (1.8) sew on the drawn rectangle and pivot carefully at the corners. Carefully cut through the very centre of the rectangle up to ½" from the ends, then cut into each corner as shown. Trim away a little of the excess batting from the cut edges. 'Post' the fabric through the letterbox you have created and through to the wrong side of the bag front. Carefully flatten and neaten the corners of the letterbox and press carefully.

6 Place the 8" zip behind the letterbox opening and baste in place with hand basting stitches or quilters double-sided ¼" tape.

7 ↓ Sew the zip neatly in place from the right side of the bag front, using a zipper foot and matching thread.

8 Working from the back of the bag front, take the second 8" square of pocket fabric and layer it right sides together with the other one, then pin the edges carefully together. Sew around the perimeter of the pocket fabrics only using a ¼" seam allowance. Do not sew through the bag front itself!

9 Make the wristlet and D ring loops. Take the 4" x 25" strip of contrast fabric and press it in half lengthways, wrong sides together. Open out the fold and turn the outer raw edges in to meet the centre crease. Press again. Now fold the whole strip down the centre crease again to form a neat folded band 1" wide. Topstitch (3.5) down both long edges of the band. Press.

10 Cut a 15" length of the band for the wristlet. Fold in a ¼" and then another ½" at both raw ends and stitch to neaten. Slip the band through a lobster/ swivel clasp, bring the short ends together, then topstitch 1" down from the neatened ends to join the wristlet into a ring. Set aside.

11 From the remaining band cut two pieces each 4" in length. Slip each one through a D ring. Position these tabs onto the back of the outer bag, 1" down from the top edge. Position the rings so they are 1" in from the side raw edge, then baste in place and trim the excess band away.

12 Make the shoulder strap in exactly the same way, but this time using a 4" x width of fabric strip of the main fabric. Neaten the raw ends but don't sew them. Slip the ends through the lobster/ swivel clasps, then sew the neatened ends in a 'box' to securely attach. Set aside for now.

13 Make the zip tabs. Take one 1¼" x 3" rectangle of contrast fabric and fold it in half, wrong sides together. Press then unfold. Now turn a ¼" in on both short ends and press to neaten. Refold down the centre. Slip the zip ends over the ends of the 10" zip and topstitch in place. You might need to adjust the length of the zip slightly so that the trimmed zip measures 11½" in total, including zip ends.

14 Interface the 10½" x 11½" bag lining pieces. Take the bag front and back and the two 10½" x 11½" lining pieces and sew them either side of the trimmed zip. After adding the front and lining, press the fabrics away from the zip and topstitch, then add the bag back and lining to the other side of the zip, sew, then press and topstitch. Open the main zip almost fully.

**15** ↓ Make the 'box bottoms' of the bag and lining. Use the Frixion pen to mark a 1½" square at the bottom of both corners on the bag front, back and both lining pieces. Carefully trim the eight squares away and discard.

**16** ↓ Bring the outer bag front and back together, right sides touching. Do the same with the bag lining front and back, and pin all around. Leave an obvious gap of 4" to 5" in the bottom seam of the lining.

**17** Sew around the bag and bag lining using a ¼" seam allowance, leaving that all-important gap for turning. Leave the box corners unsewn at this point too.

**18** ↓ Bring the side and base edges together at the corners to create the box corners and pin, then sew the four box corners, using a ¼" seam allowance.

**19** Turn the bag through to the right side and press. Bring the open edge of the lining together and hand or machine sew the gap closed.

**20** Clip the wristlet and shoulder strap onto the D rings and you are done.

Now whatever the day or date may bring, you are ready for anything!

# THE 'IT'S A DATE' BAG

**Now let's make the project using the patchwork techniques on pages 38–45.**

**BORO**

If you don't have time to hand stitch your boro, try 'matchstick' quilting in lines ¼" apart.

**IMPROV**

Save offcuts from other piecing projects, then join these together for a very quick 'improv' look.

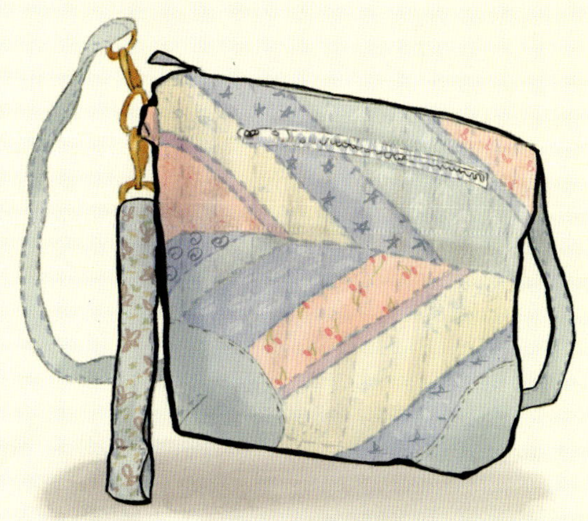

**STRING PIECE**

Create string pieced 'blocks', then join to create the bag front and back.

OPPOSITE: **HEXI**

# THE TOURIST BAG

Grab your guide book and let's go! My tourist bag is a stylish, neatly profiled crossbody number that will happily house your essentials on a day's sightseeing. The front zippered pocket is easily accessible and the main body of the bag is kept simple and roomy for your guide book and phone.

## FINISHED SIZE

9″ x 7″ x ¾″

## SKILL LEVEL

Confident beginner

## SKILLS USED

You'll use interfacing and fusible fleece, add quilting and a couple of simple zips. You'll also make loops for D rings and use webbing to create a fast and easily adjustable shoulder strap.

**Gather your supplies! You will need...**

- A fat quarter of main outer fabric
  Two 8″ x 10″ panels (portrait) for the bag back and the front zippered pocket
  Four 1″ x 3″ rectangles for the zip ends
  One 3″ x 5″ strip for the D ring loops
- 0.5m lining fabric for the lining
  Four 8″ x 10″ panels (portrait) for the bag front, front pocket lining and the bag lining
- 0.5m lightweight fusible interfacing
- 0.5m H640 or H630 fusible fleece
- Two 6″ zips
- Two ¾″ D rings
- Two ½″ swivel/lobster clasps
- One 1″ strap slider
- 55″ of 1″ wide webbing for the shoulder strap
- Threads to match your fabrics
- Frixion or fabric-safe marking pen

## LET'S MAKE THE BAG!

1 Layer each of the three 8" x 10" outer panels (two outer fabric and one lining) with a slightly larger piece of H640 fusible fleece and mark your chosen quilting design (I marked a 1" diamond crosshatch using a Frixion pen). Quilt the panels, then trim the panel you have chosen for your front zip pocket back to 8" x 10" for the time being. Leave the bag front and back panels untrimmed at this stage. Set aside.

2 Interface the front and back lining pieces with lightweight fusible interfacing, leaving the outer zipped pocket lining panel un-interfaced.

3 Make four zip ends by folding and pressing a ¼" in on both shorts ends of the 1" x 3" rectangles of outer fabric. Once this is done, fold the zip end in half, wrong sides together, so that the neatened ends match. Press. Use the zip ends to trim the ends of both zips. Make sure the zips measure 8" to 8½".

4 ↓ Cut the outer pocket quilted panel and the un-interfaced lining panel at 2½" x 8" for the pocket top and the rest of the panel (7½" x 8") for the pocket bottom.

5 ↓ Use one of the zips and both upper and lower outer zip pocket pieces and the corresponding linings to make the outer pocket. Sew the upper outer and lining to one side of the zip. Press back and topstitch, then repeat with the lower outer pocket and lining pieces. The pocket piece should still measure 8" wide; trim the length to 9½" if necessary.

6 Trim the quilted front and back bag panels to 8" x 9½". Layer the zippered pocket onto the quilted bag front panel and baste in place.

7 Use the bag front/pocket combo and one of the lining pieces. Sew these pieces to one side of the remaining zip, press the fabrics back and topstitch. Repeat with the bag back and the remaining lining piece, then press back and topstitch.

8 Make the D ring loops. Take the 3″ x 5″ piece of outer fabric and fold it in half lengthways, wrong sides together, then press. Open out the fold and bring the raw edges in to meet the centre crease. Press again.

9 ↓ Now refold down the original fold to create a ¾″ wide folded band. Topstitch down both long edges. Cut the band in half and slip each one through a D ring, then baste the raw edges together. Position the bands/D rings on the bag back, just below the main zip. Baste in place, being sure to only baste to the outer fabric, not the lining.

10 Open the main zip, then open the outer bag pieces and the lining pieces, and bring the outer bag pieces right sides together and the bag lining pieces right sides together. Pin all around.

11 ↓ Sew around the perimeter of the bag using a ⅜″ seam allowance, leaving a 4″ to 5″ gap in the lining seam for turning. Turn to the right side, then slipstitch the opening in the lining.

12 Give the bag a light press.

13 Fold the sides of one end of the webbing in by about ¼″ to taper the webbing down and sew, then pass the narrow end through one of the lobster/swivel clasps. Fold the webbing back on itself and sew securely. Pass the other end of the webbing through the strap slider, then taper the end as before. Pass this end through the remaining lobster/swivel clasp and then back through the strap slider, following general instructions on page 33 for making an adjustable strap. Sew the end of the webbing in place.

14 Attach the shoulder strap to the finished bag. Now head somewhere exciting and fabulous!

# THE TOURIST BAG

**Now let's make the project using the patchwork techniques on pages 38–45.**

### BORO

Add boro piecing to all sections of the bag. Make a large piece of 'fabric' and then cut your pattern pieces from it.

### HEXI

Small hexis look great on the bottom of this bag – add covered piping cord and strips of fabric to opposite corners for extra style!

### STRING PIECE

String piece the lower portion of the bag, piecing one way and then the other.

**OPPOSITE: IMPROV**

# THE TRAVEL BUDDY BACKPACK

My travel buddy backpack is a fantastic addition to your bag wardrobe. It's comfy to wear when travelling, walking or just on your daily commute. There's one huge zippered pocket on the front of the bag and a massive interior space too, so you really can pack a lot in. The top of the bag is also zippered and has a smart and practical rain flap to keep everything safe and dry. You can carry it on your back and it has fully adjustable shoulder straps for comfort and versatility (the straps are removable and there's a fixed carry handle at the top). I've used a smart combination of faux leather and tapestry with a cotton lining, but this bag would also look gorgeous in waxed cotton, wool tweed and faux leather, African waxed cotton, patchwork fabrics or oil cloth.

## FINISHED SIZE

14" x 14" x 3"

## SKILL LEVEL

Intermediate

## SKILLS USED

There are a number of steps and components needed to make this bag. Nothing is difficult; there are just more steps than some of the other bags in this book. Take your time, enjoy the process and, if there are any skills you need to brush up on, refer to the techniques section (see pages 22–45) to practise what you need. You'll sew a couple of simple zips, make a flap, add a magnetic snap, and make a boxed bottom and adjustable shoulder straps.

**Gather your supplies! You will need...**

- 0.5m PU/faux leather
  14½" x 12½" (landscape) for the lower bag front
  6½" x 14" (landscape) for the bag flap
- 0.5m cotton canvas or tapestry fabric
  14½" x 4½" (landscape) for the top upper bag front
  14½" x 16½" (portrait) for the bag back
- 1m cotton lining fabric
  4½" x 14½" for the front pocket upper
  14½" x 12½" for the front pocket lower
  Three 14½" x 16½" rectangles for the front pocket lining and the bag lining
  One 6½" x 14" rectangle for the flap lining
- Two 16" long #5 zips with one zip pull attached to each
- Four 1" D rings
- Four 1" swivel/lobster clasps
- Two 1" strap sliders
- 3m of 1" wide nylon webbing
  Two 40" lengths for the shoulder straps
  One 16" length for the loop reinforcement
  One 9" length for the carry handle
  Four 3" lengths for the D ring attachments (use a lighter to seal the ends of the webbing after you cut it to length)

*Continues overleaf*

## LET'S MAKE THE BAG!

1 ↓ Make the flap. Layer the outer flap and lining pieces and use a small round object to round the lower two corners. Interface the wrong side of the flap lining. Find the centre point of the flap lining and measure 1″ up from the bottom edge. Position and fit the male half of the magnetic snap here.

2 Place the flap lining and flap outer, right sides together, and sew around the sides and base, leaving the top open. Notch the curved edges and turn to the right side. Press or use a seam roller to flatten the edges. Topstitch the sides and baste the open top of the flap. Set aside.

3 Make the front zip pocket and the bag front. Sandwich one side of a zip between the outer front pocket upper and the front pocket upper lining. Sew using a zipper foot. Press the outer and lining away from the zipper and press, then topstitch close to the zipper. Find the centre of the pocket upper and measure 1″ up from the zip. Mark and fit the female half of the magnetic snap here, making sure you only go through the outer fabric, and the lining covers the back of the snap.

*Continues overleaf*

- 6″ x 13½″ medium-weight interfacing for the bag flap
- One magnetic snap
- Threads to match your project
- A lighter (optional)
- 505 basting spray (optional)
- Quilters/sewing clips and pins
- Small round object for rounding the flap corners
- Zipper foot
- Walking foot or non-stick foot is useful when sewing faux leather
- Seam roller

4 ↓ Repeat this process with the outer and lining lower sections of the front pocket (no magnetic snap here though!) and the other side of the zip. (In my bag this section is faux leather, so I used a seam roller rather than an iron to press, and I used a walking foot to do the topstitching.) Baste the whole front zippered pocket to one of the 14½" x 16½" lining pieces. You may need to trim a little off the bottom of the front pocket so that it fits the lining perfectly.

5 ↓ Make the bag back. Working at the top of the front outer panel, measure 4½" in from each side and place a pin. Position the carry handle here and baste in place. Position the bag flap over the carry handle, right sides together (the flap is not as wide as the bag back). Make sure it sits centrally, then baste the flap into position. Thread a D ring through a 3" piece of webbing and baste the raw edges together. Make four. Position one D ring/loop either side of the carry handle approximately 1" down from the flap seam. Baste in place. Layer the reinforcement length of webbing over the raw edges and topstitch in place.

6 Mark and cut a 1½" square from the lower corners of the bag back. Now measure up 1" from these. Cut away the corners and place a D ring/loop here. Baste, then repeat on the other side of the bag.

7 ↓ Mark and cut away 1½" lower corners on the bag front and both main lining pieces too.

8 ↓ Sew the main zip in place. Grab the remaining zip, the bag front, bag back and the main inner lining pieces. Sew the zip in place between the bag back and one lining piece first. Press the lining and outer bag away from the zip, then together, then topstitch very close to the bag flap on the main back fabric. Sew the other side of the zip to the bag front and the other lining piece. Press back and topstitch close to the zip.

9 Make sure the main zip is half open. Open the lining pieces away from the main bag and bring the lining to the lining and the outer bag to the outer bag. Pin or clip carefully, then sew around the perimeter of the bag, leaving a 6″ gap in the bottom of the lining for turning.

10 ↓ Turn the bag through to the right side and push out the corners carefully. Sew the gap in the lining by hand or machine.

11 ↓ Make the adjustable shoulder straps. Take one 40″ length of webbing and push one end through a swivel clasp. Fold up the lower 2″ of the webbing and stitch in place. Thread a strap slider onto the webbing, then thread the end of the webbing through another swivel clasp. Loop the end of the webbing back under the T bar of the strap adjuster, then sew the raw end of the webbing back on itself. Make a second adjustable strap in the same way (see page 33 if you're not sure how!).

12 Clip the adjustable shoulder straps onto the backpack and you are ready for an adventure!

# THE TRAVEL BUDDY BACKPACK

**Now let's make the project using the patchwork techniques on pages 38–45.**

**BORO**

Divide the backpack up into three sections. Add boro to the outer ⅔ of the main bag and the inner ⅓ of the flap.

**HEXI**

Make the bag flap from small hexi pieces. Lots of impact from just a little hand piecing!

**STRING PIECE**

Create the whole bag from string piecing but work the panels in opposite directions.

**OPPOSITE: IMPROV**

# THE VOYAGER

This is my absolute must-have bag when I'm going anywhere and everywhere. Even though I may take another bag with me, the voyager is always included. It's the perfect size for my wallet, phone, cards and keys, and best of all I can wear it under a jacket or coat without disturbing the look of my clothes, so it's the perfect security bag for travelling or for festivals too.

## FINISHED SIZE

5″ x 7″ x ½″

## SKILL LEVEL

Intermediate/advanced

## SKILLS USED

This bag is a little trickier to make because of that very narrow gusset and hand-stitched lining. You'll also make a simple pocket, attach a press stud or KAM snap, insert a zip around corners and make a narrow shoulder strap with a strap slider.

**Gather your supplies! You will need...**

- A fat quarter of main outer fabric
  One 5½″ square for the bag back
  One 5½″ x 9½″ panel (portrait) for the front pocket and lining
  One 1½″ x 5½″ rectangle (landscape) for the front top band
  One 2″ x WOF (42″) strip for the shoulder strap
  One 2″ x 5½″ rectangle (portrait) for the security flap

- A fat quarter of contrast outer fabric
  Three 1½″ x 5½″ strips for the upper and lower bands (landscape)
  One 5½″ x 6½″ rectangle for the bag front
  One 1″ x 12″ strip for the gusset
  One 3″ x 5″ strip for the D ring loops
  One 2″ x 5½″ rectangle for the security flap lining

- A fat quarter of lining fabric
  Two 5½″ x 7½″ rectangles
  Three 1″ x 12″ strips for the gusset

- Threads to match your fabrics, and thread to closely match your zipper tape, plus an appropriate hand-sewing needle

- 0.25m medium-weight fusible interfacing

- Two ¾″ D rings

- Two ½″ lobster/swivel clasps

- One ½″ strap slider

*Continues overleaf*

BRITISH PASSPORT

## LET'S MAKE THE BAG!

**Use ¼" seam allowances throughout**

1 ↓ For the bag back, sew a 1½" x 5½" contrast strip to the top and bottom of the 5½" square of main fabric. Press and topstitch near the seams. Interface the back panel.

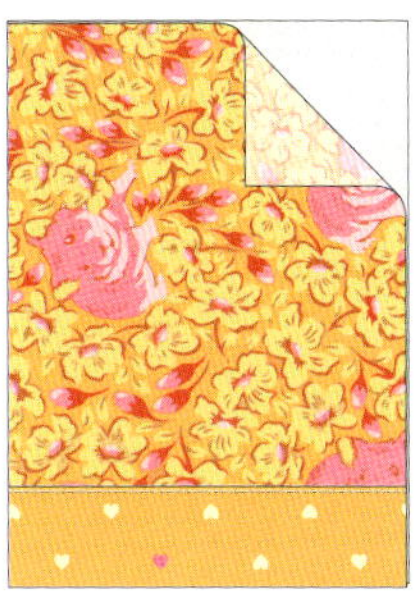

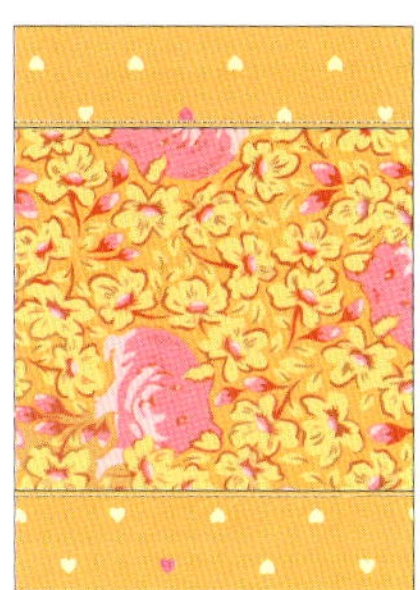

2 Make the bag front. Sew the 1½" x 5½" strip of main fabric to the 5½" x 6½" panel of contrast fabric. Press and topstitch near the seam, then interface the bag front.

3 ↓ Make the front pocket. Sew the remaining 1½" x 5½" strip of contrast fabric to the bottom edge of the 5½" x 9½" pocket piece. Interface the pocket piece, then fold it in half, wrong sides together, and topstitch near to the fold at the top and also next to the seam on the contrast strip. Mark a dot on the pocket 1" down from the top edge, centred. Apply one half of the KAM snap or press stud. Baste the pocket to the bag front.

*Continues overleaf*

- One matching KAM snap set in a toning colour plus fitting tools, or substitute a small sew-on snap fastener or press stud
- One 12" zip to match your fabrics
- Frixion or fabric-safe marking pen
- Small round object for rounding the flap corners

4 ↓ Make the security flap. Interface the 2″ x 5½″ strip of main fabric on the wrong side. Layer it, right sides together, with the 2″ x 5½″ contrast strip, then use a small round object to round off the lower corners. Trim to the drawn line.

5 Sew around the security flap, leaving the short edge open for turning. Turn to the right side, push out the curve smoothly and press. Mark a dot centrally, 1″ up from the curved edge, for the snap/press stud. Apply the second half of the KAM snap or press stud to the centre of the curved edge. Baste the security flap to the centre of the bag back.

6 Make the D ring loops. Take the 3″ x 5″ strip of contrast fabric and press it in half down the length, wrong sides together. Open out the fabric and turn the raw edges into the middle crease and press again. Finally, refold the strip down the centre fold to create a ¾″ folded strip. Topstitch either side of the strip. Cut the strip into two 2½″ lengths, thread each one through a D ring and match the raw ends, then baste. I also like to sew very close to the D ring itself using a zipper foot to get very close. This stops the D ring slipping and sliding around on the finished bag. Baste the D rings/loops either side of the security flap on the bag back.

7 ↓ Use a small round object to slightly round off the four corners of both the bag front and back. Trim to the curved line.

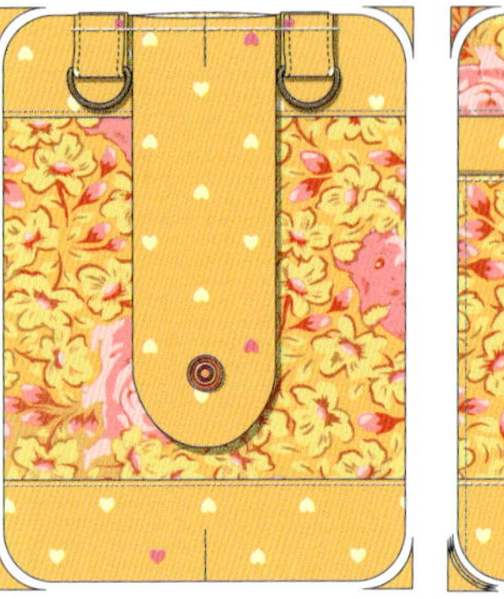

8 Mark the centre at the top and bottom on both the bag front and back.

9 ↓ Make the gusset. Sew the zip and the 1″ x 12″ gusset strip together to make a circle. Mark the centre of the zip and the centre of the gusset strip with a dot using a fabric-safe pen. Open out the zip. Carefully pin the zip/gusset around the bag front, matching the centre marks on the gusset and zip with the corresponding marks on the bag front. Sew the gusset and zip to the bag front, clipping into the gusset fabric and zip tape a little to help you around the curves.

10 ↓ Repeat the process with the bag back. Make sure the flap and D ring loops are tucked inside as you sew.

11 Turn the bag out to the right side and gently press, then turn it inside-out again.

12 Make the shoulder strap. Take the 2" x WOF main fabric strip and interface the whole thing on the wrong side. Fold it as you did the strip for the D ring loops. Also fold in the short raw ends to neaten, then topstitch on all four sides. Thread the strap through a lobster/swivel clasp and sew the strap in place with a 'box'. Thread the other end through the strap slider and then through the second lobster/swivel clasp, following general instructions on page 33. Sew the end of the strip in place.

13 Make the lining. Take one of the 1" x 12" gusset pieces and fold it in half, wrong sides together, and press to make a ½" x 12" strip. Repeat once more. Carefully lay these strips together so that the folded edges just touch and baste the ends together – this will line either side of the zip.

14 Now sew the remaining 1" x 12" strip of gusset fabric to the zip lining pieces to create a circle. Round off the corners of the front and back lining as before, then sew the gusset/zip lining pieces to the lining front and then the back. Snip into the gusset seam allowance if you need to in order to get smooth curved corners. Turn the lining right-side out.

15 ↓ Place the outer bag inside the lining, wrong sides together. Carefully match the zip cover to the zip, paying particular attention to the start and finish of the zip opening. Use thread that matches the zip and hand sew the lining to the zip tape to cover the construction seam. Don't attach the lining too close to the zip so that it upsets its smooth running. Use tiny hand stitches.

16 Turn the bag through to the right side and give it a final press, making sure to avoid the KAM snap when ironing.

17 Attach the shoulder strap using the lobster/swivel clasps and adjust the shoulder strap to fit!

# THE VOYAGER

**Now let's make the project using the patchwork techniques on pages 38–45.**

**HEXI**
A few ½" hexis look proportionate used just on the top of this bag.

**IMPROV**
Use your smallest scraps to piece half square triangles and strips.

**STRING PIECE**
Focus your string piecing on just the pocket area.

**OPPOSITE: BORO**

# THE 'WORK, REST AND PLAY' BAG

This bag is such a great all-rounder – that's why I've called it the Work, Rest and Play! There's a roomy interior, the handles allow easy opening of the bag to gain full access, and it has two side pockets stitched into the gusset. I've used trapezoid-shaped acrylic handles, but you could use D-shaped or circular too. Try using bamboo or wooden handles – there are lots of possibilities to give this bag a fresh new look!

## FINISHED SIZE

13″ x 12″ x 4″

## SKILL LEVEL

Intermediate

## SKILLS USED

You'll use a paper pattern, do some quilting, make pockets and add a quilt-style binding, sew a curved gusset, make a drop-in lining and sew in an acrylic or bamboo handle.

**Gather your supplies! You will need...**

- 0.5m of main outer fabric (A) for the bag front and back, and also the side pockets
- 0.25m of contrast outer fabric (B) for the gusset
- 2½″ x 12″ of accent fabric (C) for the pocket binding
- 0.5m of lining fabric
- Quilt batting/wadding for the bag front, back and gusset
- Fusible medium-weight interfacing for the pockets
- Thread to match
- A pair of acrylic/plastic/wooden handles (mine have a 4½″ aperture, but slightly smaller would work perfectly well)
- Frixion or fabric-safe marking pen
- Pattern piece for the bag and pockets (see pullout template sheet)

## LET'S MAKE THE BAG!

1 Use the pattern piece for the front/back to cut a front and back from outer fabric A and also a front and back from the lining fabric. From fabric A also cut two pocket pieces, and from the lining fabric cut two pocket pieces also.

2 From contrast fabric B cut one 5" x 29½" strip of fabric for the bag gusset. Cut the same size piece from the lining fabric.

3 From accent fabric (C) cut two 2½" x 6" pieces of fabric for the pocket bindings.

4 From the quilting wadding/batting cut a bag front and bag back, cutting the wadding ¼" smaller on the sides and base and using the 'fold line' as your upper cut line, thus the wadding is 3" shorter than the outer and lining fabrics and will sit within the seam allowances. From the wadding also cut one 4½" x 29" strip for the gusset.

5 From the fusible interfacing cut two pocket pieces.

6 Layer the wadding onto the wrong side of the bag front and back and then the wrong side of the gusset. Quilt as desired (I quilted a 2" diamond crosshatch on the front/back panels and a vertical line ⅜" apart on the gusset).

7 → Interface the outer pocket pieces, then layer the outer with a lining, right sides together. Sew across the bottom of the pocket with a ¼" seam allowance, turn to the right side and press. Baste the top and side edges together within the seam allowance. Fold one 2½" x 6" strip of accent fabric in half lengthways and use to bind the top edge of the pocket. Trim the excess binding from the ends. Make two.

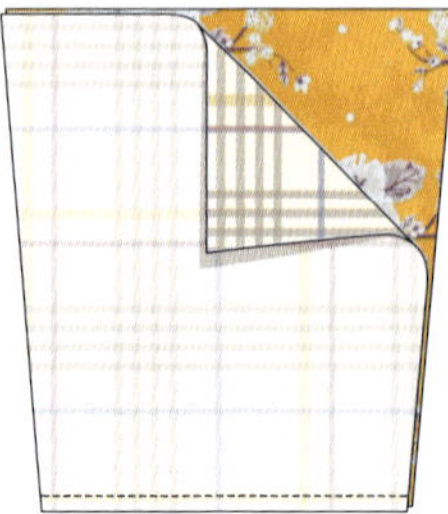

8 ↓ Position the pockets 1½" down from the ends of the gusset, making sure that the bound edge is nearest the ends of the gusset. Pin the bottom edge in place and then topstitch. Bring the side edges of the pocket to meet the raw edges of the gusset; this will cause the top, bound edge of the pocket to pop outwards. Pin in place, then baste close to the edge. Repeat at both ends of the gusset.

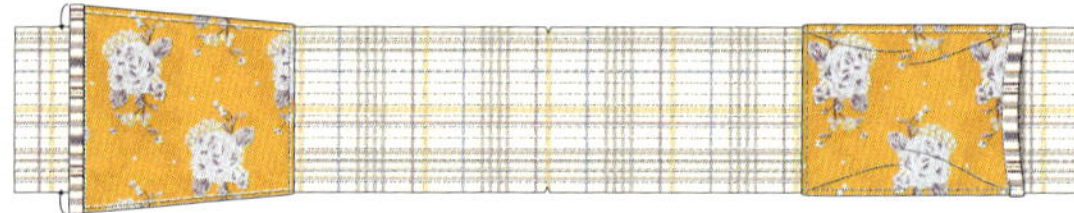

9 → Find the centre points of the bag front and the gusset and mark with a fabric-safe pen or with a small notch snipped into the fabric. Match the centre points, then pin the gusset to the bag front. Sew the gusset in place, starting and finishing sewing ⅜" down from the top raw edge. Sew with a ¼" seam allowance. Repeat with the other side of the gusset, making sure that the top of the gusset is level on both sides before sewing. Use lots of pins and take your time!

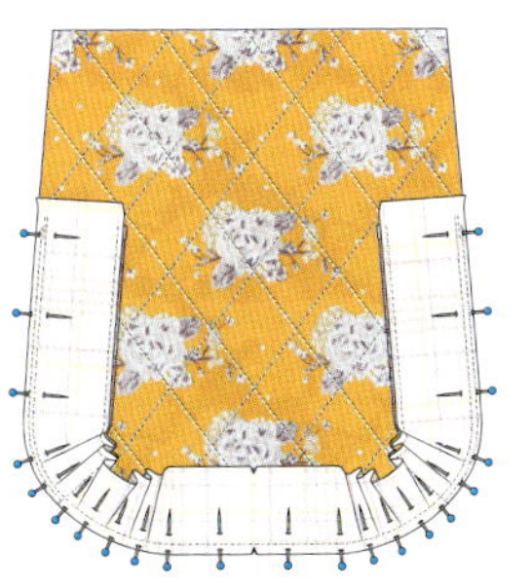

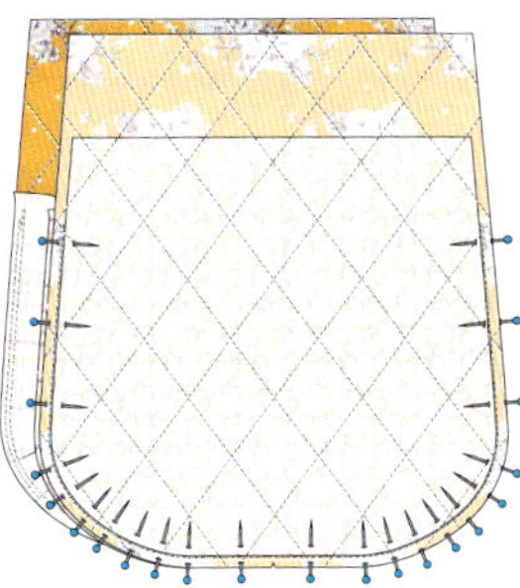

**10** Make the lining in exactly the same way, starting and finishing your stitching ⅜" down from the top edges. You could add a simple patch pocket to the lining if you wish, but if you do, be sure to position it at least 4" down from the top raw edge.

**11** ↓ Press a generous ¼" seam allowance in on all the raw edges of both the outer bag and the lining. Turn the outer bag right-sides out and drop the lining into the bag. Match all the edges up very neatly and pin from the front. Topstitch from the front very close to the neatened edge. Press the bag, fold the top 3" down on both sides of the opening and press. Use a fabric-safe pen to mark where the folded edge sits.

**12** ↓ Take one of the handles and position it on the wrong side of the bag, wrap the first part of the bag top over the handle and bring it to meet the marked line. Start to topstitch the fabric in place, enclosing the handle. Keep folding a little more of the bag over and stitching down – there shouldn't be any pleats or tucks in your sewing, but the fabric will naturally gather along the handle as you sew. Keep sewing until you get to the end of the fabric and backstitch at the end to secure. Repeat with the other side of the bag and the other handle.

And that's it! You're done! Now you're ready for anything ... work, rest or play!

# THE 'WORK, REST AND PLAY' BAG

**Now let's make the project using the patchwork techniques on pages 38–45.**

**HEXI**
Large hexis look great on just the main front panel of this bag.

**IMPROV**
Create a wide band of improv piecing, then add wide plain strips to the sides before cutting the main bag front and back.

**STRING PIECE**
Create small 'blocks' of string piecing. Join them, then cut the main bag front and back.

OPPOSITE: **BORO**

# THE 'YOGA ON THE BEACH' BAG

This is a giant of a bag ... big enough to fit all your supplies for a day at the beach or your workout change of clothes if you're heading to a yoga class. But why not combine the two and do yoga on the beach? There's a deep and secure zippered pocket on the back of the bag for your valuables, and a 'sling' across the front to slip your yoga mat or beach towel into. The side panels feature magnetic snaps – these are optional but give the bag the ability to fold inwards, creating a very different profile and a bit of added security. This is a very useful pattern to use and adapt. Leave off the sling if you wish and make a second back panel, with or without the zippered pocket. It also makes a great shopper or bag to take to quilt class!

## FINISHED SIZE

16″ x 15″ x 8″

## SKILL LEVEL

Confident Beginner

## SKILLS USED

You'll do some quilting, put in a simple sling with tabs, add magnetic snaps, sew a 'box' bag and sew in a lining with faux binding.

**Gather your supplies! You will need...**

- 0.5m of main fabric A for the front sling, back zippered pocket and side panels
- 0.5m of fabric B for the front accent panels and the main back panel
- 0.5m of fabric C for the sling lining and bag lining
- 2m of 1½″ wide webbing for the handles
- One 7″ piece of #5 zip and a #5 zip pull, or a regular 7″ zip
- Threads to match your fabrics
- Bosal In-R-Form fusible foam
- Medium-weight fusible interfacing
- Frixion or fabric-safe marking pen
- Two magnetic snaps

## LET'S MAKE THE BAG!

1 Use a fabric-safe pen to label the pieces of foam and interfacing as you go along, otherwise you'll end up with lots of mystery white rectangles!

2 From the Bosal-In-R Form fusible foam cut two 16" x 15" rectangles for the bag front and back, two 8" x 15" rectangles for the bag sides, and one 8" x 16" rectangle for the bag base.

3 From the fusible interfacing cut two 16" x 15" rectangles for the lining front and back, two 8" x 15" rectangles for the lining sides, one 8" x 16" rectangle for the bag base, one 8" x 15" rectangle for the sling, one 4" x 8" rectangle for the zippered pocket top and one 8" x 11"rectangle for the zippered pocket bottom.

4 ↓ Make the front of the bag. From main fabric A cut one 8½" x 15½" rectangle for the sling front. From lining fabric C, cut a piece to the same size and interface it. Place the outer and lining right sides together and sew down the long sides using a ¼" seam allowance. Turn to the right side, press and topstitch the long ends. Set aside.

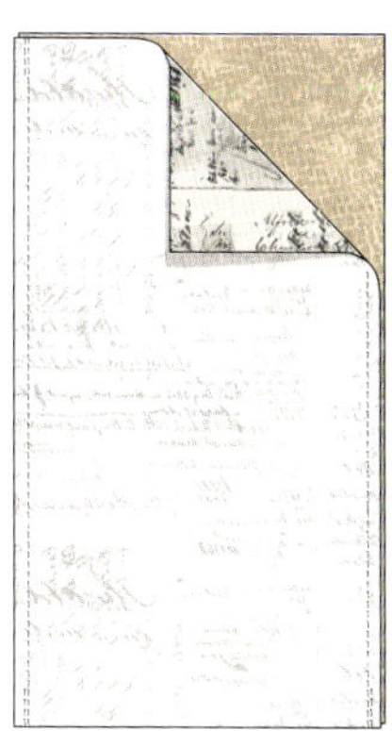

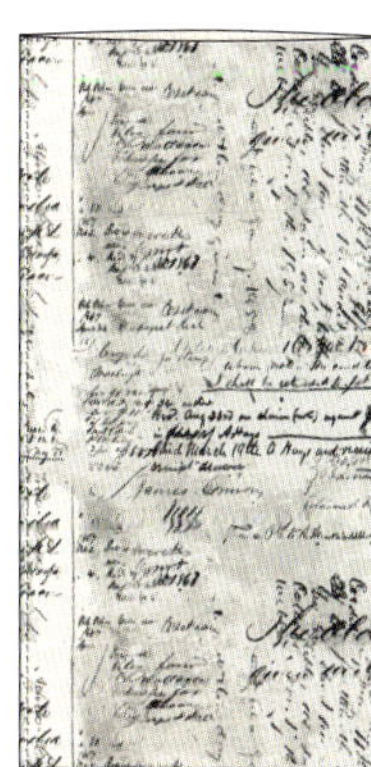

5 ↓ From fabric B cut a 16½" x 15½" panel (landscape) and fuse it to the corresponding piece of foam. Mark your quilting and quilt as desired (I marked a 2" diagonal grid, quilted on the lines, then quilted a second set of lines ⅜" away from the first to create a very smart 'double crosshatch'). When the quilting is completed, remove your lines, layer the sling on top of the front panel, sling centred, and baste in place at the top and bottom. Set aside the front panel.

6 Make the back panel. Start with the zippered pocket. From main fabric A cut an 4½" x 8½" panel (landscape) for the pocket top and one 8½" x 11½" panel for the pocket bottom. Cut the same sized pieces from lining fabric C and interface these lining pieces with the appropriate pieces of interfacing.

7 From lining fabric C cut two 2" x 4" rectangles for the zip ends. Fold ¼" in on each short end and press. Fold the rectangle in half so that the folded ends are level, then press. Use to cover the ends of the zip and stitch in place.

8 Layer the zip with the outer upper and lining pieces, and sew in place using a zipper foot. Press open and topstitch. Repeat with the lower parts of the pocket. Trim the lower edge so that the whole zippered pocket measures 8½" x 15½".

*Continues overleaf*

9 From lining fabric C cut an 8½" x 15½" panel. Baste the zippered pocket to this panel.

10 ↓ From fabric B cut two 4½" x 15½" panels (portrait). Sew these panels either side of the basted zippered pocket using a ¼" seam allowance. Press. Fuse this 16" x 15" panel to the corresponding piece of Bosal foam. Add some quilting to the contrast panels and topstitch either side of the pocket. Sew a line across the upper edge of the pocket top approximately ½" from the top of the zip. Set the back panel aside.

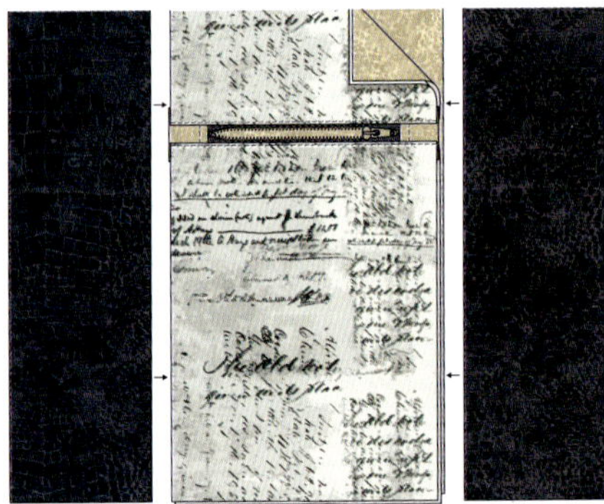

11 Make the side and base panels. From main fabric cut two 8½" x 15½" rectangles (portrait) and from lining fabric C cut one 8½" x 16½" base panel. Fuse the fabrics to the corresponding pieces of foam. Quilt as desired (I quilted diamond crosshatch on my panels but played with scale a little: a 1½" diamond in the side panels and a 2" crosshatch in the base).

12 ↓ Fit the magnetic snaps to the side panels (if using). Mark the centre line on the panel top, measure 1½" out from this centre line to both the left and right and mark these two lines. Measure 2" down from the top and place marks to indicate the position of the snaps. Fit the male and female halves of the snap at these points. Repeat on the other side panel.

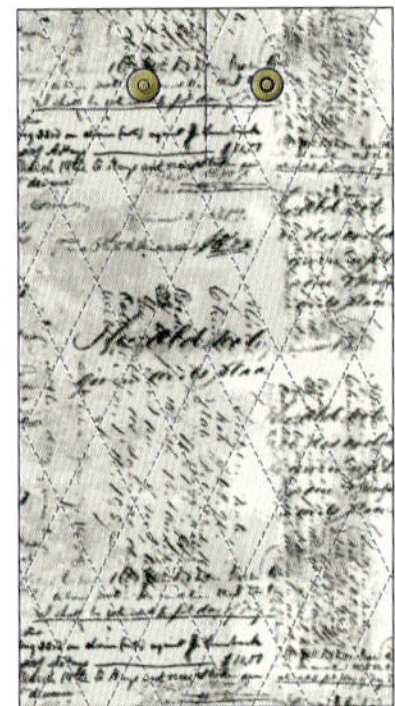

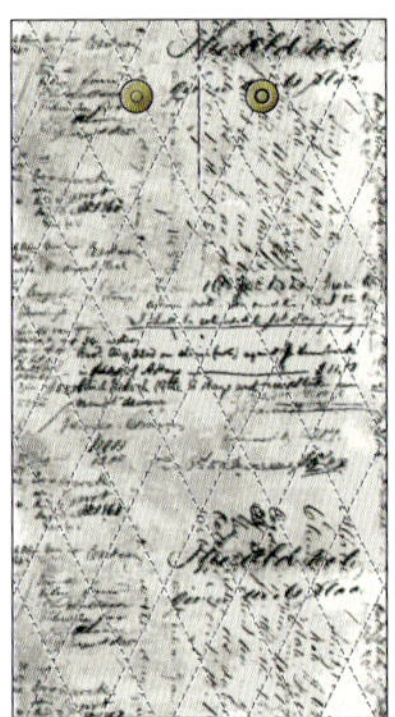

13 → Lay out your front, back, base and side panels as shown. Sew the panels together using a ¼" seam allowance. When sewing to or from a corner, start and finish your sewing ¼" in from the edge, and backstitch to secure. Sew the base to the bag front and back first, sew the sides in place and then finally the side/base seams.

14 Turn the bag to the right side and press.

15 ↓ Sew the handles on. Cut two 34″ lengths from the webbing. Mark a line 2″ down from the top of the bag either side of the zippered pocket or sling. Position the raw ends of the webbing against these marks, with the handles hanging down, and sew in place. Now flip the handles up, covering the raw ends of the webbing (a bit like a French seam) and sew in place securely with a 'box'. Repeat for all four ends of the handles.

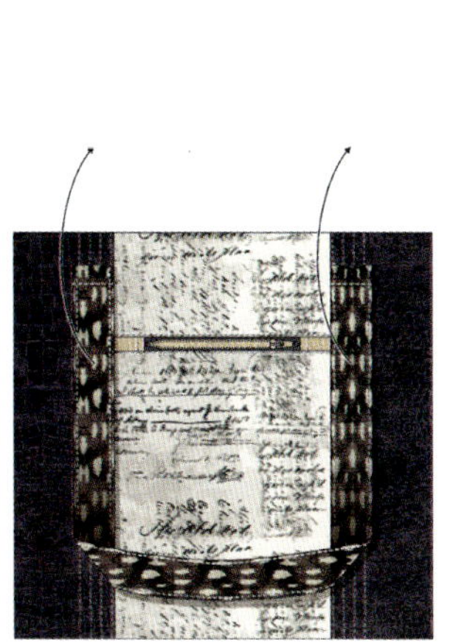

16 Make the lining. From lining fabric C cut two 16½″ x 15½″ panels, two 8½″ x 15½″ panels, and one 8½″ x 16½″ panel. Interface all panels. Sew the lining as you did the exterior, but leave a 5″ gap in the base seam for turning.

17 ↓ Sit the outer bag inside the lining and pin the top edges together. Sew around the top of the bag using a ⅜″ seam allowance. Turn the bag to the right side and press.

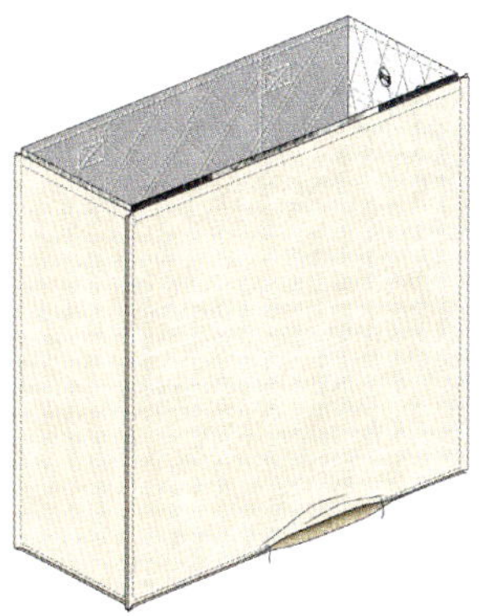

18 Slipstitch the opening in the lining closed.

19 Push the lining into the bag, but allow the top ¼″ to remain visible from the right side, forming a 'faux' binding.

20 Topstitch from the front, in the ditch between the main bag and the 'binding'. Give the bag a final press, then decide where your first outing should be. Yoga on the beach anyone?

# THE 'YOGA ON THE BEACH' BAG

**Now let's make the project using the patchwork techniques on pages 38–45.**

**BORO**

Focus boro piecing on the sides of the bag only.

**HEXI**

Combine large and small hexis in one project with this bag. Use every scrap!

**STRING PIECE**

Use string piecing on the side sections – piece the string sections at a 45° angle in opposite directions.

**OPPOSITE: IMPROV**

# THE 'WIDE AND SASSY' BAG

A perfect stylish bag for daytime adventures. You could easily add a removable shoulder strap or fabric handles to change up the look of this bag. I've used a combination of Bosal In-R-Form to provide structure on the outside, and medium-weight interfacing on the lining for a smart and defined profile inside and out. I've included a twist lock, which is quick to apply but could easily be replaced with a button/hole or a magnetic snap if you prefer.

## FINISHED SIZE

12" x 10" x 4"

## SKILL LEVEL

Beginner

## SKILLS USED

You'll use fusible foam, do some quilting, make a simple box bag and make a flap. You'll also insert a twist lock (optional) and sew on ready-made handles.

**I have shown two versions of this bag: one made with 0.5m of fabric and one using fat quarters to show how you could mix up the fabrics.**

**Gather your supplies! You will need...**

- 0.5m main patterned fabric or two fat quarters of complementary fabrics

**For the bag front and back**

- Fat quarter of contrast fabric for the sides, base, handle loops and flap
- 0.5m plain cotton for the lining
- 0.5m medium-weight fusible interfacing
- 0.5m single-sided fusible In-R-Form or fusible foam
- Two bag handles with 4½" aperture and ½" slots for loop attachments
- One twist lock or magnetic snap
- Threads to match your fabrics
- Small round object, such as a small dish, to round the corners of the flap

## LET'S MAKE THE BAG!

1 From the In-R-Form foam and interfacing cut two 10½" x 12½" rectangles for the bag front and back, two 4½" x 10½" rectangles for the bag sides, and one 4½" x 12½" rectangle for the base. From In-R-Form only, cut one 4½" x 8½" rectangle for the flap.

2 From the lining fabric cut two 10½" x 12½" rectangles, two 4½" x 10½" rectangles and one 4½" x 12½" rectangle.

3 From the main fabric cut two 10½" x 12½" rectangles (landscape) for the front and back panels. Alternatively, if you are using two fat quarters of complementary fabric, from one of them cut two 6½" x 10½" rectangles (portrait), and four 3½" x 10½" rectangles (portrait) from the second fat quarter. Sew a 3½" x 10½" rectangle either side of the 6½" x 10½" rectangle to make a 10½" x 12½" panel (landscape). Make two and then proceed with the pattern.

4 From the contrast outer fabric cut two 4½" x 10½" rectangles, one 4½" x 12½" rectangle, and two 4½" x 8½" rectangles (for the outer and lining of the flap).

5 Interface the lining pieces – front and back, two sides and base – using the fusible interfacing.

6 Fuse the outer bag front and back, both sides and the base to the corresponding pieces of In-R-Form foam. Quilt these pieces as desired.

7 ↓ Fuse one of the flap pieces to the foam, Quilt as desired, then use a round object to round the bottom edge and trim to shape. Layer with the remaining flap piece, rights sides together. Sew around the sides and lower curved edge using a ¼" seam allowance, leaving the top edge open. Turn to the right side and press, then topstitch on all sides.

8 Measure 2" up from the lower curved edge and install the outer part of the twist lock (if using). Set aside.

9 Make the outer bag by sewing the base, then the sides of the outer bag to the front and back. Start by sewing the base to the bag front, starting and finishing the seams ¼" in front the edge. Sew the back onto the base in the same way.

10 ↓ Now add the sides, laying a bag side onto the bag front, right sides together. Sew right from the top but stop ¼" before the bottom edge. Sew the side piece to the bag back, then sew across the base edge. Repeat on the other side of the bag. Turn the bag to the right side and press all seams: this forms a neat 'box'-style bag.

11 → Find the centre back of the outer bag and baste the flap in place.

12 Find the centre front of the outer bag and measure 5" down from the top of the bag. Install the other part of the twist lock here.

13 Repeat the outer bag-making process with the lining, but leave a 4" to 5" gap in one of the base seams for turning. Leave the lining wrong-sides out.

**14** Insert the outer bag into the lining and pin or clip the top edges together, making sure the flap and handles are tucked inside! Sew around the top of the bag using a ⅜″ seam allowance. Turn the bag through the gap in the lining, then close the gap by hand or machine.

**15** Press the top edge of the bag and topstitch ¼″ down from the top.

**16** ↓ Sew on the leather/PU handles either side of the flap, approximately 3″ in from the side edges and approximately 1″ down from the top edge.

**17** ↓ Optional last step (this gives the bag a more rounded profile). Turn the bag inside out and pinch the side edge together. Measure 1″ in from the centre and 3″ down the side. Mark a line and sew this 'dart'. Repeat on the other side of the bag. Turn through to the right side and press.

You're done!

## THE 'DEEP AND MEANINGFUL' BAG

You can very easily make this bag into more of a shopper tote by increasing the depth of the front and back panels and the side pieces.

**18** Cut 14½″ x 12½″ front and back panels (portrait) and two 4½″ x 14½″ side panels. Do this in outer fabric, lining fabric, interfacing and In-R-Form foam. Everything else remains the same. You could add a patch/slip pocket inside; just make sure you set it low enough not to interfere with sewing on the handles. One change makes a huge difference!

# THE 'WIDE AND SASSY' BAG

**Now let's make the project using the patchwork techniques on pages 38–45.**

**BORO**

Focus the boro on the bag sides and flap.

**IMPROV**

Add improv quilting to the bag sides and flap.

**HEXI**

Concentrate your hexi piecing on the centre panel for lots of impact (and not a lot of hand piecing).

**OPPOSITE: STRING PIECE**

# BAG-MAKING MEASUREMENTS

STYLING: 12–14″ (30–35.5cm)

⅛″ (3mm)
¼″ (6mm)
⅜″ (1cm)
½″ (1.3cm)
⅝″ (1.6cm)
¾″ (1.9cm)
1″ (2.5cm)
1¼″ (3.2cm)
1½″ (3.8cm)
1¾″ (4.4cm)
2″ (5cm)
2¼″ (5.7cm)
2½″ (shown as 6.2cm or 6.4cm)
2¾″ (7cm)
3″ (shown as 7.6cm or 8cm)
3¼″ (8.3cm)
3½″ (8.9cm)
3¾″ (9.5cm)
4″ (10.2cm)
4¼″ (10.8cm)
4½″ (11.5)
5″ (shown as 12.7cm or 13cm)
5½″ (14cm)
6″ (shown as 15cm or 15.2cm)
6¼″ (15.9cm)
6½″ (16.5cm)
7″ (17.8cm)
7½″ (19cm)
8″ (20.3cm)
8½″ (21.6cm)
9″ (23cm)
9¼″ (23.5cm)
9½″ (24cm)
9¾″ (0.25m)
10″ (shown as 25cm or 25.4cm)
10¼″ (26cm)
10½″ (26.7cm)
11″ (28cm)
11½″ (29.2cm)
12″ (30cm)
12½″ (31.8cm)
13″ (33cm)
13½″ (shown as 34cm or 34.3cm)
14″ (35.5cm)
14½″ (36.8cm)
15″ (38.1cm)
15½″ (39.4cm)
16″ (40.6cm)
16½″ (42cm)
17″ (43cm)
17½″ (44.5cm)
18″ (shown as 45.7cm or 46cm)
18½″ (47cm)
19¾″ (0.5m)
20″ (50.8cm)
20½″ (52cm)
21″ (shown as 53cm or 53.3cm)
21½ (54.6cm)
22½″ (57.2cm)
24″ (61cm)
25″ (63.5cm)
28″ (71cm)
29½″ (shown as 73.7cm or 0.75m)
30″ (shown as 76cm or 76.2cm)
32″ (81.3cm)
33″ (83.9cm)
34″ (86cm)
34½″ (87.6cm)
35½″ (shown as 90cm or 90.2cm)
36″ (91.4cm)
38″ (96.5)
39½″ (1m)
40″ (102cm)
42″ (shown as 106.7cm or 107cm)
44″ (shown as 111.8cm or 112cm)
48″ (122cm)
49″ (1.25m)
50″ (127cm)
53″ (134cm)
54″ (shown as 137cm or 137.2cm)
56″ (142cm)
58″ (1.5m)
59″ (shown as 150cm or 1.5m)
60″ (shown as 152cm or 152.4cm)
60½″ (153.7cm)
61″ (155cm)
64″ (162.6cm)
66″ (167.6cm)
78¾″ (2m)
80″ (203cm)
84″ (213cm)
98″ (2.5m)
126″ (3.2m)

2¼ yd (2m)
3¼ yd (3m)
5½ yd (5m)

# RESOURCES

## SEWING MACHINES

**Brother Sewing Machines**
www.sewingcraft.brother.eu/en

## LONGARM QUILTING MACHINES

**HandiQuilter**
www.handiquilter.com

**UK-dedicated retailer for HandiQuilter**
www.pinholequilting.co.uk

## SEWING MACHINE NEEDLES

**Schmetz**
www.schmetz.com

## HAND-SEWING NEEDLES

**John James Needles**
www.jjneedles.com

## MACHINE SEWING, HAND SEWING AND QUILTING THREADS

**Gütermann threads**
www.consumer.guetermann.com

## INTERFACINGS/STABILISERS/FUSIBLE FOAM

**Bosal (for fusible In-R-Form foam and a range of interfacings)**
www.bosalfoam.com

**Vliesofix (for interfacings, volume fleece, quilt batting, Style-Vil fusible foam, waist shaper and Decovil)**
www.vlieseline.com

## FABRICS/BAG-MAKING EQUIPMENT/ INTERFACINGS AND FOAM

**Amazon**
www.amazon.com

**Bramble Patch**
www.bramblepatchonline.com

**Deany Fabrics**
www.deanyfabrics.co.uk

**Doughty's**
www.doughtysonline.co.uk

**Empress Mills**
www.empressmills.co.uk

**Hobbycraft (for general sewing supplies, bag-making hardware and fabrics)**
www.hobbycraft.co.uk

**John Lewis (for bag-making metalware, interfacings, general sewing supplies and fabrics)**
www.johnlewis.com

**Lady Sew and Sew**
www.ladysewandsew.co.uk

**Oh Sew Sweet**
www.ohsewsweetshop.co.uk

**Sewing Street (website and dedicated sewing and soft craft TV channel)**
www.sewingstreet.com / Freeview 73, Sky 670, Virgin Media 754

**The Cotton Patch**
www.cottonpatch.co.uk

## ZIP JIGS

**Emi B Designs**
www.emibdesigns.co.uk

# ACKNOWLEDGEMENTS

*Make 100 Bags* has been a huge project and one I could never have done alone. Firstly I'd like to give heartfelt thanks to my publisher, Laura Russell, for having such faith in me to write another book and for her unwavering support in all of my projects. Thanks also to the wonderful team at Pavilion who brought so much talent and enthusiasm to this book: to Alice, Shamar, Daisy and Lily ... and also to Rachel Whiting whose exquisite photography and knack of knowing just how to show every project at its absolute best, is unparalleled. Thanks to Kang Chen and Virginia Romo who brought such life to the illustrations and did an amazing job of turning my ideas, thoughts and wild hand gestures into diagrams and fashion plates which look incredible!

Thank you to my wonderful agent, Elly, and also to Rob at HHB agency, who guide, support and keep the wheels turning. I cherish working with you all. A massive thank you to all at *Sewing Street*, but particularly Jess, Hayley and Scott who made sure I had access to the most fabulous array of bag-making tools, fabrics and hardware ... and also to Brother Sewing Machines, who supplied a beautiful machine for the shoot but also for supplying the incredible Brother sewing machine that I used to sew, quilt and create every one of the bags in this book.

I owe a huge debt of gratitude to friends who helped with the sewing. Hilary made much of the English paper pieced fabrics, and her nimble fingers and gorgeous colour sense absolutely shine in her projects; Joan made most of the Boro fabrics in the book, and I am in awe of Joan's artistic talents and creativity – you are both my cherished sewing sisters.

Thank you to Joan, Shamar, Daisy and Alice for modelling throughout the book; it might not be in anyone's job title, but you all rose magnificently to the task and were delightful to work with.

Thank you Charlie ... my cherished husband and soul mate. You never waver in your support and encouragement, and you help me every day to be the best version of myself.

And finally thank you to everyone who buys my books, enjoys what I do and encourages me to do more. You are the reason I put pen to paper and thread to fabric; you are all the reason and the motivation for everything I do. Let's enjoy this wonderful creative journey together!